To Jean

from Donald

with love

April 1979

Edward Thomas on the Countryside

also by Edward Thomas

COLLECTED POEMS OF EDWARD THOMAS

SELECTED POEMS OF EDWARD THOMAS

Edward Thomas on the Countryside

A Selection of his Prose and Verse

edited by
ROLAND GANT

FABER AND FABER
3 Queen Square
London

First published in 1977
by Faber and Faber Limited
3 Queen Square London WC1
Printed in Great Britain by
Latimer Trend & Company Ltd Plymouth
All rights reserved

ISBN 0 571 10799 0

Contents

৵ঞ৸

FIGURES IN THE LANDSCAPE

THROUGH THE YEAR

Introduction

On the flyleaf of an algebra book, 'perhaps not quite without ostentation, in the worst possible Latin', Edward Thomas wrote: 'I love birds more than books.'

Then a new boy at his public school, Saint Paul's, he was ill at ease, ashamed of his skinniness and too shy to mix and play Rugby with his fellows. He was often bored—'I suppose there were never duller books than Bright's *England*, Kitchin's *France*, Lodge's *Europe*, anybody's *Political Economy*'—and found escape in reading about travel and nature and in studying maps. Most of all he loved walking in the country, listening to and identifying birds, observing the shifting patterns of light, shade and clouds and, like Richard Jefferies, recording in a notebook what he saw. Jefferies was his favourite writer and he even read his books over buns in an empty class-room rather than join the lunchtime clatter and discussion.

Born on 3rd March 1878, his childhood was spent 'at peace with life', the eldest of six brothers brought up by a mother whose singing enthralled him and a father whose eloquence impressed him. In the hope that Edward would follow him into the Civil Service and reach a higher grade than he himself held at the Board of Trade, his father had him coached in Latin and Greek in preparation for the public school's entrance examination. To Edward, Herodotus and Ovid were 'nuisances' when he 'was thinking all the time about Jefferies . . .'. But there were plenty of books in the Thomases' house and when he was fifteen he used to read, re-read and recite Tennyson's 'The May Queen'. 'I enjoyed the beauty of spring mixed with the sadness of death' he wrote in *The Childhood of Edward Thomas*, and it was in the spring of 1917 that he was killed by shell-blast at Arras at the age of thirty-nine.

While at school he began writing essays and one of them so impressed James Ashcroft Noble, a neighbour and literary critic, that he invited him to his house. This meeting was of great importance in Thomas's life. Not only did Noble encourage him in his writing and use his influence to get his first book, *The Woodland Life*, published when he was nineteen, and introduce him to the work of writers new to him, but it was Noble's second daughter Helen who became his wife while he was still an undergraduate at Oxford.

Edward decided to live by writing which, apart from being a bitter disappointment to his father, set him on a course of ceaseless work to earn a meagre living for himself, Helen, and their three children. In spite of lack of money, constant insecurity and frequent housemoving, Edward Thomas fulfilled punctiliously whatever he undertook, whether reviewing (Dr R. G. Thomas estimates that Thomas wrote a million words in just over a decade) or writing books ranging in subject from *Feminine Influence on the Poets*, *Windsor Castle*, biographies of Lafcadio Hearn and Maeterlinck to those nearer his heart like *The Life of Richard Jefferies* and *The South Country*. His scholarship was formidable and his patience and conscientiousness never failed him although much of what he did was literary drudgery that pinioned his creative impulse, chaining him to chair, table and lamplight, and raising what Helen Thomas called his 'demon of melancholia', that reflective Celtic brooding which had come to him with his Welsh blood. Sedentary toil, near poverty and mental exhaustion often drove him to slam the cottage door behind him and, bearing the torment of guilt and remorse 'walk far into the night, and come home worn out with deadly fatigue' (Helen Thomas).

Thomas alleviated his spiritual loneliness by walking. For him the road was 'a silent companion always ready for us, whether it is night or day, wet or fine, whether we are calm or desperate, well or sick. It is always going: it has never gone right away, and no man is too late. Those bouts of anguish resulting from what Helen Thomas called his 'strange complex temperament' were accepted by her with the unflinching patience and strength that she drew from her love for him. Although he could enchant his listeners at Oxford and later delight friends who visited him in the country he considered that 'social intercourse is only an intense form of solitude' and he never shook off his sense of isolation. 'It is a commonplace that each of us is alone, that every piece of ground where a man stands is a desert island with footprints of unknown creatures all round its shore.' And he said 'I always walk alone.' In childhood he had already begun to 'hate crowds and societies and grown-up people' and preferred being alone to enjoy the 'lovely visible earth and sky and sea' or a wood 'companionable . . . reassuring to the solitary'. He said that a wood gave him a feeling of ease and seclusion—an unequivocal statement of his need for isolation. In addition to that acute perceptiveness that made him one of the greatest English writers on nature I suspect that he put aspects of himself into characters he encountered and wrote about to humour some of his traits and air certain self-doubts in his search for a degree of reconciliation between his contemplative side and the inescapable reality of life.

Jung, who was three years older than Thomas, explained in *Memories, Dreams and Reflections* that 'somewhere deep in the background I always knew I was two persons' and Thomas similarly felt the need to project himself into his double, 'Philip', to whom he referred later as 'the child whom I used to know better than I have known anyone else'. During four years of his boyhood Edward shared with his silent companion 'Philip' the 'supernaturally beautiful' landscape of 'Our Country'. 'Again and again Philip and I revisited that lane of larches, the long waterside copse, the oak wood out in the midst of the fields, and all the hedges, to find moorhen's eggs, a golden-crested wren's nest and a thousand treasures and felicity itself.'

There are some striking parallels between the boyhood personalities of Thomas and Jung. Jung was 'remote from the world of men, but close to nature, the earth, the sun, the moon, the weather, all living creatures.' They shared a dislike of school and a detestation of conventionality, Thomas's hatred of 'stiff Sunday streets, stiff Sunday clothes and Sunday hats, black clothes and silk hats and neatly folded umbrellas and shining walking-sticks' echoing Jung's 'it seemed to me that the high mountains, the rivers, lakes, trees, flowers and animals far better exemplified the essence of God than men with their ridiculous clothes. . . .'

This is not an attempt to fit Edward Thomas and his thinking and behaviour into a neat slot of 'interpretation'. He did, however, refer to himself as 'a strong citizen of infinity and eternity' in 'The Stile' and the final paragraph of that essay shows his awareness of the personal and collective unconscious in the Jungian sense.

Few of Thomas's poems were published in his lifetime and general recognition of their quality was slow in coming but when it did it pushed his prose works into the background. With the exception of a few reissues as volumes in series, his books have been neglected for half a century and dismissed often as mere bread-and-butter work by a poet who was enabled to blossom only when his soldier's pay released him from wage-earning. He spoke of himself as 'a writing animal' and he was objectively aware of the 'aesthetic' mannerisms and stylistic devices fashionable in his Oxford days, and the preciosity and occasional verbosity which marked his early work. But he moved steadily towards simplicity in his prose, 'as near akin as possible to the talk of a Surrey peasant' he told his brother Julian. He was trying, he informed Eleanor Farjeon, 'to get rid of the last rags of rhetoric and formality which left my prose so often with a dead rhythm'. This was the poet speaking, of course, and the quality of Thomas's prose lies very much in his poet's feeling for the sound and music of words, immediately apparent when reading him aloud.

In a small over-populated island choking on its own industrialization, there is a growing wish to experience open spaces, even vicariously. Edward Thomas's prose and poetry about the English countryside remain vividly fresh and he reminds us that there was a time when poppies 'so desirable in their serenity' still coloured our cornfields. When he was a child Thomas could find 'real country' just outside Clapham or Wandsworth—'I had no idea that London died in this way into the wild', but later he wrote of 'the irresistible enemy that is drawing its lines invisibly and silently about (the city) on every side'. He saw that same enemy advancing on Welsh towns where 'every inch of the soil was covered with bricks, stones, cement, asphalte, iron-work, granite blocks. Not a tree or blade of grass was allowed to appear anywhere but in the graveyards, and even there the earth was plated almost entirely with tombstones. They were afraid of leaving any space unguarded lest Nature should show a regret, a curse or a warning.'

So there was pollution as well as the poppy in 1909 and when Edward Thomas came into contact with the industrial wasteland and the population brutalized by it he wrote with a desperate and savage power that recalls D. H. Lawrence on the subject. Now, when poppies have been sprayed nearly out of existence but an effort has been made to check pollution, there is a hunger for 'country writing' among the inhabitants of the sprawling urban fortresses. Some of that writing is as artificial as the plastic thatch tacked on the roofs of weekend cottages and as inappropriate as the ploughs and village pumps pilloried on suburban lawns. And how scathing Edward Thomas would be about the 'rustick' pub's wall-to-wall Sunday morning clientele getting back to nature over gin-and-tonic and instant county guides in which adjectives such as 'quaint' and 'picturesque' are distributed by their sponsored compilers like stars in a good-food guide.

Thomas would have welcomed the National Trust and the action of local authorities as, for example, at Swindon where Coate Farmhouse has a Jefferies museum and the land around Coate Water—where Thomas's uncle taught him to fish—has been made a municipal park. My own extensive walking has sometimes led me along the same tracks over downs, fells and mountains as those followed by Edward Thomas over sixty years and two wars ago. I often wonder what he would have thought of the changes that have taken place in the landscape. Some are depressing, like pylons, and some are for the better, such as underground telephone cables, and nearly all are inevitable. The London to South Wales motorway slices within a mile of the game-keeper's cottage where Edward and Helen spent their honeymoon. But the cottage is still as it is described in *As It Was* and the couple who have lived there for most of the years of this century and with whom I have talked in the kitchen where Dad and Granny Uzzell danced and sang with the Thomases, are country people. Tramping from there along the Ridgeway in early spring the only man I met was the driver of a mud-bound tractor beyond whom the battlements of the Atomic Energy Research Establishment gleamed on the horizon like a gigantic mythological castle. And when I was walking alone over the Quantocks I saw outlined against the Bristol Channel the twin towers of Hinkley Point nuclear power station, raised like a minster of the New Atomic Church.

The changes that Edward Thomas would notice most of all are probably ecological. The felling of trees, during World War I in particular, was followed by extensive afforestation. In many places conifers have been brought in where none grew before and this has produced changes in the plant and animal life there. Timber that shored up trenches and dugouts in France often came from woods where English birds had sung and nested and then, deprived, moved on.

During his final months in France Edward Thomas kept a diary, cryptic notes but explicit enough to convey that solitude, once cherished but which for the first time he did not and could not welcome. Yet, surrounded by desolation, he could still find brief delight in the 'chilled clear air' and his ear and mind were receptive to the birds he had always loved, the blackbird 'singing in the quiet of the battery' and the larks in no man's land whose song he was intent on hearing in spite of the shelling as he went above ground in the early light.

At the beginning of this introduction I said that while at school Edward Thomas had written, with a kind of defiance, 'I love birds more than books'. Throughout his life birds and the country brought him joy and inspired much of his best work and the writing and reading of books gave him pleasure as well as a living. Twenty-five years after making that declaration, amid the death-soaked mud at Arras in April 1917, he wrote on the last page of his diary:

> The light of the new moon and every star
> And no more singing for the bird.

ROLAND GANT

Acknowledgements

I wish to thank Myfanwy Thomas for permission to reprint passages from *The Childhood of Edward Thomas* and from her father's *Diary 1 January–8 April, 1917* which first appeared in *The Anglo-Welsh Review, Autumn 1971,* and for proof-reading this volume.

I am also grateful for their critical advice and comments to Nadia Legrand, William Cooke and Paul Scott and for help in tracing and lending me books to Sally Muir, Mervyn Horder, Christopher Radmall and Douglas Matthews of the London Library.

ROADS AND
FOOTPATHS

On Roads and Footpaths

Much has been written of travel, far less of the road. Writers have treated the road as a passive means to an end, and honoured it most when it has been an obstacle; they leave the impression that a road is a connection between two points which only exists when the traveller is upon it. Though there is much travel in the Old Testament, 'the way' is used chiefly as a metaphor. 'Abram journeyed, going on still toward the south,' says the historian, who would have used the same words had the patriarch employed wings. Yet to a nomadic people the road was as important as anything upon it. The earliest roads wandered like rivers through the land, having, like rivers, one necessity, to keep in motion. We still say that a road 'goes' to London, as we 'go' ourselves. We point out a white snake on a green hill-side, and tell a man: 'That is going to Chichester.' At our inn we think when recollecting the day: 'That road must have gone to Strata Florida.' We could not attribute more life to them if we had moving roads with platforms on the side-walks. We may go or stay, but the road will go up over the mountains to Llandovery, and then up again over to Tregaron. It is a silent companion always ready for us, whether it is night or day, wet or fine, whether we are calm or desperate, well or sick. It is always going: it has never gone right away, and no man is too late. Only a humorist could doubt this, like the boy in a lane who was asked: 'Where does this lane go to, boy?' and answered: 'I have been living here these sixteen years and it has never moved to my knowledge.' Some roads creep, some continue merely; some advance with majesty, some mount a hill in curves like a soaring seagull.

Even as towns are built by rivers, instead of rivers being conducted past towns, so the first settlements grew up alongside roads which had formerly existed simply as the natural lines of travel for a travelling race. The oldest roads often touch the fewest of our modern towns, villages, and isolated houses. It has been conjectured that the first roads were originally the tracks of animals. The elephant's path or tunnel through the jungle is used as a road in India today, and in early days the wild herds must have been invaluable for making a way through forest, for showing the firmest portions of bogs and lowland marshes, and for suggesting fords. The herd would wind according to the conditions of the land and to inclinations of many inexplicable kinds, but the winding of the road would be no disadvantage to men who found their living by the wayside, men to whom time was not money. Roads which grew thus by nature and by necessity appear to be almost as lasting as rivers. They are found fit for the uses of countless different generations of men outside cities, because, apart from cities and their needs, life changes little. If they go out of use in a new or a changed civilization, they may still be frequented by men of the most primitive habit. All over England may be found old roads, called Gypsy Lane, Tinker's Lane, or Smuggler's Lane; east of Calne, in Wiltshire, is a Juggler's Lane; and as if the ugliness of the 'uggle' sound pleased the good virtuous country folk, they have got a Huggler's Hole a little west of Semley and south of Sedgehill in the same county: there are also Beggar's Lanes and roads leading past places called Mock Beggar, which is said to mean Much Beggar. These little-used roads are known to lovers, thieves, smugglers, and ghosts. Even if long neglected they are not easily obliterated. On the fairly even and dry ground of the high ridges where men and cattle could spread out wide as they journeyed, the earth itself is unchanged by centuries of traffic, save that the grass is made finer, shorter, paler, and more numerously starred with daisies. But on the slopes down to a plain or ford the road takes its immortality by violence, for it is divided into two or three or a score of narrow courses, trenched so deeply that they might often seem to be the work rather of some fierce natural force than of slow-travelling men, cattle, and pack-horses. The name Holloway, or Holway, is therefore a likely sign of an old road. So is Sandy Lane, a name in which lurks the half-fond contempt of country people for the road which a good 'hard road' has superseded, and now little used save in bird's-nesting or court-ing days. These old roads will endure as long as the Roman streets, though great is the difference between the unraised trackway, as dim as a wind-path on the sea, and the straight embanked Roman highway which made the proverb 'Plain as Dunstable Road', or 'Good plain Dunstable'—for Watling Street goes broad and straight through that town. Scott has one of these ghostly old roads in *Guy Mannering*. It was over a heath that had Skiddaw and Saddleback for background, and he calls it a *blind road*—'the track so slightly marked by the passengers' footsteps that it can but be traced by a slight shade of verdure from the darker heath around it, and, being only visible to the eye when at some distance, ceases to be distinguished while the foot is actually treading it.'

The making of such roads seems one of the most natural operations of man, one in which he least conflicts with nature and the animals. If he makes roads outright and rapidly, for a definite purpose, they may perish as rapidly, like the new roads of modern Japanese enterprise, and their ancient predecessors live on to smile at their ambition. These are the winding ways preferred by your connoisseur today. 'Give me,' says Hazlitt, 'the clear blue sky over my head and the green turf beneath my feet, a winding road before me, and a three-hours' march to dinner—and then to thinking!' These windings are created by the undulating of the land, and by obstacles like those of a river—curves such as those in the High Street of Oxford, which Wordsworth called 'the stream-like windings of that glorious street'. The least obstacle might bring about a loop, if nothing more, and as even a Roman road curled round Silbury Hill, so the path of the Australian savage is to be seen twisting round bush after bush as if it enjoyed the interruption, though it cannot purl like the river at a bend. Probably these twists, besides being unconsciously adapted to the lie of the land, were, as they are still, easeful and pleasant to the rover who had some natural love of journeying. Why go straight? There is nothing at the end of any road better than may be found beside it, though there would be no travel did men believe it. The straight road, except over level and open country, can only be made by those in whom extreme haste and forethought have destroyed the power of joy, either at the end or at any part of its course. Why, then, go straight? The connoisseur had something of the savage in him when he demanded a winding road.

The Icknield Way

Roads

I love roads:
The goddesses that dwell
Far along invisible
Are my favourite gods.

Roads go on
While we forget, and are
Forgotten like a star
That shoots and is gone.

On this earth 'tis sure
We men have not made
Anything that doth fade
So soon, so long endure:

The hill road wet with rain
In the sun would not gleam
Like a winding stream
If we trod it not again.

They are lonely
While we sleep, lonelier
For lack of the traveller
Who is now a dream only.

From dawn's twilight
And all the clouds like sheep
On the mountains of sleep
They wind into the night.

The next turn may reveal
Heaven: upon the crest
The close pine clump, at rest
And black, may Hell conceal.

Often footsore, never
Yet of the road I weary,
Though long and steep and dreary,
As it winds on for ever.

Helen of the roads,
The mountain ways of Wales
And the Mabinogion tales
Is one of the true gods,

Abiding in the trees,
The threes and fours so wise,
The larger companies,
That by the roadside be,

And beneath the rafter
Else uninhabited
Excepting by the dead;
And it is her laughter

At morn and night I hear
When the thrush cock sings
Bright irrelevant things,
And when the chanticleer

Calls back to their own night
Troops that make loneliness
With their light footsteps' press,
As Helen's own are light.

Now all roads lead to France
And heavy is the tread
Of the living; but the dead
Returning lightly dance:

Whatever the road bring
To me or take from me,
They keep me company
With their pattering,

Crowding the solitude
Of the loops over the downs,
Hushing the roar of towns
And their brief multitude.

Collected Poems

The Ridgeway
ᴀᴥᴥᴩ

Best of all the Down ways is the Ridgeway, joining it where it crosses the Hungerford road or near Chisledon. Jefferies knew it well; this above all others would take him past 'hill after hill and plain and plain' in silence and solitude. It passes under Liddington Hill, with little risings and fallings through the open corn-land, but, climbing almost to Barbury Castle, it keeps a great height along the top of Hackpen Hill, paving itself with harebell, silverweed, eyebright and bartsia; now east now west, now south, it commands vast soaring and diving grounds for the delighted eyes, among solitary slopes of green and white hills, of turf and cloud. Moles, journeying often in the grassy ruts, turn up a fine dark soil from above the chalk. Tumuli, earthworks, and ancient settlements, and flocks of 'grey wethers' or sarsen stones, mark the side of the road until it dips to East Kennett, across the Bath Road, and on to Alton Priors over Wansdyke, which it intersects at Furze Hill. Wansdyke, that stupendous highway and barrier, running from near Heddington Wick over Morgan's Hill, by Shepherd's Shore, over Tann Hill to Savernake Forest, makes a rough southern boundary to the country of Jefferies, except that it excludes part of the forest. If the Ridgeway is left on Avebury Down, another grassy track leads into Avebury; and most pleasant is the descent among the sarsens that rest on turf blue with sheep's-bit or rosy with rest-harrow. Jefferies knew Avebury, through love of the Down ways and through his early archaeological curiosity. What they worshipped at Avebury Temple no one knows, but the human mind is still fertile in fantasy and ferocity—if it no longer draws blood—when it worships within walls. To me the sycamores that gloom at the entrance to the temple are more divine. The village, built partly of roughly hewn, worn sarsen, is enclosed among the temple's huge upright stones that make some such impression as a Celtic shore.

Almost parallel with the Ridgeway is the road from Swindon to Avebury and Devizes, joined from Coate by way of Ladder Hill and Wroughton village. Jefferies had friends at Wroughton, and must have known the church above the beeches, with its Sadlers, Codringtons, Benets, and Stubbeses, dead in battle, in child-bed, in peace, lying sententiously with coats of arms, skulls, scrolls, the vine, crowns, cross-bones, and epitaphs, to commemorate them; the churchyard also (with some gipsy tombs), where gravestones lean this way and that, to suggest a battlefield of fallen and falling and still unwounded men. Jefferies, in an early paper, quoted Aubrey's praise of this country as the 'garden of Wiltshire', and tried to show that the Battle of Ellandune was fought near by in 823. Beyond the church, the road goes south-westward between banks of saw-wort, scabious, bedstraw, and yarrow, bounding the corn. Wherever there is a slope, it is trenched deep by a road, used or not. The telegraph-posts go ahead, with something of adventure in their persistency, their silent and lean serviceableness. A crawling cider-press passes on its way to Wootton Bassett, in charge of three young men, a boy, and an old man with peeled staff. Hackpen is in sight; between the road and the hill corn waves and sheep tinkle at the sainfoin; three beautiful slender ploughs stand alone in the midst of the long, hedgeless undulations, while the wind blows the smoking rain. Here, as along many of the Down roads, grows the meadow crane's-bill, which Jefferies loved—a flower whose purple has wedded passion's opulence and thought's tranquillity. Broad Hinton, the next village on this road, fills a considerable space in Jefferies' earliest descriptions; he mentions the small white horse on the downside near the church, the mansion which its owner burned to save from the Parliament in the Civil War, and the legendary treasure in a well close by. The church was described again in an early anonymous paper in the *Graphic*. (At 'The Bull' here a labourer says that a farmer at Braden still bakes lardy cakes once a fortnight, and loaves of which four would cover the inn table.) Broad Hinton Church is off the main road, but is on a track which runs from Bincknoll Camp southward until the white road takes its place just before Avebury Temple. For a large part of its way it runs alongside of a winterbourne that rises in Uffcott Down and feeds the Kennet. This track should be followed from Broad Hinton churchyard, whereby it enters the fields near beeches and a moated farm, and then straight over pink and white yarrow flowers, through the wheat to Winterbourne Bassett church tower, that stands among elms and beeches, thatched long barns and stacks and the marks of rased buildings; a stone circle lies within a mile. Just beyond the church a farmhouse has a peacock as a weathercock. Berwick Bassett Church, on the same path, is but a mile beyond, small and low, with mellow tiles and a little spire upon its tower—the whole dwarfed by great barns and ash-trees. Winterbourne Monkton, where the track joins the road, is nearly all thatched, and the walls are made largely of rude pieces of sarsen. Avebury Down and the 'grey wethers' rise close on the east, domed Windmill Hill and its tumuli on the west. Wansdyke is not far south, reached past Silbury Hill and Beckhampton, and a rookery that is perched a mile from any house in a wood of elm, ash, oak, and fir.

The Life of Richard Jefferies

Birds of a Feather Flock Together

Before the winter was at an end little Bob Dumpling of Dumpling Green in Norfolk, started westward to see his father, who was at Glastonbury in Somerset. A drover from Thetford was taking some cattle as far as Salisbury, and from there had to go on to Ilchester to fetch a hundred sheep. He promised to have the boy along with him as far as Warminster, where he would hand him over to the first man going to Glastonbury. So Bob took to the road with the drover. It was that green road that guides men across England into the west. The daisies of the short turf were still covered up in frost, but in among the cattle the air was like spring, because they kept away the wind and their breath was both warm and sweet. If Bob got tired, the drover, whose name was Davy, carried him. Thus it was on Davy's shoulders that the boy first saw the towns of England—Newmarket, Royston, Dunstable, Watlington, Wantage—evening after evening. In the clear hard weather men were ploughing in the Thames valley below them as they passed by. The earth was turned up in rich, dark clods like the inside of a frosted cake, and on to the furrows descended hundreds of white gulls. When Bob shouted, the birds rose up and whirled in the air like snow. Wherever the fields had been striped black by the plough there was a dappling of white gulls on the black.

The high downs on their left hand were white, but often dotted or blotched with black rooks. In the wayside thorn-bushes flitted scores of yellow-hammers as bright as flowers on the bare branches. 'Birds of a feather flock together,' said Bob. ''Tis true, lad,' said Davy, 'though I never heard it before. 'Tis poetry, too. Some people are born to make poetry. Now, I have a little lass just gone two years old, and one day she sees a sparrow hopping close to the door and says to me: "What is it?" and says I: "A little cock sparrow," and what do you think she says? Well, she says: "Sat on a sallow". A little cock sparrow sat on a sallow. That's poetry. But it isn't true. He wasn't on a sallow, but she doesn't know a sallow from an oak. But it's poetry, and so is yours:

> Birds of a feather
> Flock together.

I like that. Besides, 'tis true.'

So man and boy and cattle crossed over the downs and came into Salisbury. There Davy left his cattle and got drunk for the night. Bob slept in the cathedral, as Davy had told him to do, and was awakened by the clergy and the choir coming in all in white.

> Birds of a feather
> Flock together,

said Bob, staring at them from his hiding-place. Outside the cathedral, as he sat waiting for Davy, he saw the black clergy-birds flocking together here and there, just as jackdaws did overhead on the tall spire and in the blue sky.

Davy came at last with four other drunken drovers.

'Here's Bob Dumpling, the poet,' said he to them. 'Say the poem, Bob.'

> Birds of a feather
> Flock together,

said Bob. 'True,' said one of the drovers, 'for we be all lovers of Joan's ale, and though we be not birds, yet I think the ale gives us wings to find one another.' Davy said that he had to take care of the poet, and the others went off to scatter abroad the poem in all the ale houses.

Bob was quickly at Warminster, but two days passed before a man could be found going to Glastonbury. In these two days somebody had got ahead of him: for the first words he heard in Glastonbury were the two lines of his poem. A man was telling a story outside the George Inn. Everybody laughed at the end of it, except one, who turned away very sagely, saying:

> Birds of a feather
> Flock together.

Bob met his father safely and in due time returned to Norfolk, but though he lived to be ninety-three he never made another poem; and so many people made out it was theirs, or nobody's, that neither he himself, nor Davy the drover, was believed, when they said that he was the author; and he was buried in a grave without a stone, nobody knows where.

Four-and-Twenty Blackbirds

The Green Roads

The green roads that end in the forest
Are strewn with white goose feathers this June,

Like marks left behind by someone gone to the forest
To show his track. But he has never come back.

Down each green road a cottage looks at the forest.
Round one the nettle towers; two are bathed in
    flowers.

An old man along the green road to the forest
Strays from one, from another a child alone.

In the thicket bordering the forest,
All day long a thrush twiddles his song.

It is old, but the trees are young in the forest,
All but one like a castle keep, in the middle deep.

That oak saw the ages pass in the forest:
They were a host, but their memories are lost,

For the tree is dead: all things forget the forest
Excepting perhaps me, when now I see

The old man, the child, the goose feathers at the
    edge of the forest,
And hear all day long the thrush repeat his song.

Collected Poems

Crossroads
ᕦᴥᕤ

A crossing of roads encloses a waste place of no man's land, of dwarf oaks, hawthorn, bramble and fern, and the flowers of knapweed and harebell, and golden tormentil embroidering the heather and the minute seedling oaks. Follow one of these roads past straight avenues of elms leading up to a farm (built square of stone, under a roof of thatch or stone slate, and lying well back from the road across a level meadow with some willows in the midst, elms round about, willow herb waving rosy by the stream at the border), or merely to a cluster of ricks; and presently the hedges open wide apart and the level white road cools itself under the many trees of a green, wych elms, sycamores, limes and horse-chestnuts, by a pool, and, on the other side, the sign of the 'White Hart', its horns held back upon its haunches. A stone-built farm and its barns and sheds lie close to the green on either side, and another of more stateliness where the hedges once more run close together alongside the road. This farmhouse has three dormers, two rows of five shadowy windows below, and an ivied porch not quite in the centre; a modest lawn divided by a straight path; dense, well-watered borders of grey lavender, rosemary, ladslove, halberds of crimson hollyhock, infinite blending stars of Michaelmas daisy; old apple trees seeming to be pulled down almost to the grass by glossy-rinded fruit: and, behind the bended line of hills a league away, wedding the lowly meadows, the house and the trees to the large heavens and their white procession of clouds out of the south and the sea. The utmost kindliness of earth is expressed in these three houses, the trees on the flat green, the slightly curving road across it, the uneven posts and rails leaning this way and that at the edge of the pond. The trees are so arranged about the road that they weave a harmony of welcome, of blessing, a viaticum for whosoever passes by and only for a moment tastes their shade, acknowledges unconsciously their attitudes, hears their dry summer murmuring, sees the house behind them. The way-farer knows nothing of those who built them and those who live therein, of those who planted the trees just so and not otherwise, of the

causes that shaped the green, any more than of those who reaped and
threshed the barley, and picked and dried and packed the hops that
made the ale at the 'White Hart'. He only knows that centuries of peace
and hard work and planning for the undreaded future have made it
possible. The spirit of the place, all this council of time and Nature and
men, enriches the air with a bloom deeper than summer's blue of
distance; it drowses while it delights the responding mind with a magic
such as once upon a time men thought to express by gods of the hearth,
by Faunus and the flying nymphs, by fairies, angels, saints, a magic
which none of these things is too strange and 'supernatural' to represent.
For after the longest inventory of what is here visible and open to an-
alysis, much remains over, imponderable but mighty. Often when the
lark is high he seems to be singing in some keyless chamber of the
brain; so here the house is built in shadowy replica. If only we could
make a graven image of this spirit instead of a muddy untruthful
reflection of words! I have sometimes thought that a statue, the statue
of a human or heroic or divine figure, might more fitly than in many
another stand in such a place. A figure, it should be, like that benign
proud Demeter in marble now banished to a recess in a cold gallery,
before which a man of any religion, or class, or race, or time might
bow and lay down something of his burden and take away what makes
him other than he was. She would be at home and blithe again, enshrined in the rain or in this flowery sunlight of an English green, near
the wych elm and sycamore and the walls of stone, the mortar mixed,
as in all true buildings, with human blood.

The South Country

The Stile

Three roads meet in the midst of a little green without a house or the
sign of one, and at one edge there is an oak copse with untrimmed
hedges. One road goes east, another west, and the other north; southward goes a path known chiefly to lovers, and the stile which transfers
them to it from the rushy turf is at a corner of the copse.

The country is low, rich in grass and small streams, mazily sub-
divided by crooked hedgerows, with here and there tall oaks in broken
lines or, round the farm houses, in musing protective clusters. It is

walled in, by hills on every side, the higher ones bare, the lower furred with trees, and so nearly level is it that, from any part of it, all these walls of hills, and their attendant clouds can be seen.

I have known the copse well for years. It holds an acre of oaks two or three generations old, the roots of ancient ones, and an undergrowth of hazel and brier which is nearly hidden by the high thorn hedge.

One day I stopped by the stile at the corner to say good-bye to a friend who had walked thus far with me. It was about half an hour after the sunset of a dry, hot day among the many wet ones in that July. We had been talking easily and warmly together, in such a way that there was no knowing whose was any one thought, because we were in electrical contact and each leapt to complete the other's words, just as if some poet had chosen to use the form of an eclogue and had made us the two shepherds who were to utter his mind through our dialogue. When he spoke I had already the same thing in the same words to express. When either of us spoke we were saying what we could not have said to any other man at any other time.

But as we reached the stile our tongues and our steps ceased together, and I was instantly aware of the silence through which our walking and talking had drawn a thin line up to this point. We had been going on without looking at one another in the twilight. Now we were face to face. We wished to go on speaking but could not. My eyes wandered to the rippled outline of the dark heavy hills against the sky, which was now pale and barred with the grey ribs of a delicate sunset. High up I saw Gemma; I even began trying to make out the bent star bow of which it is the centre. I saw the plain, now a vague dark sea of trees and hedges, where lay my homeward path. Again I looked at the face near me, and one of us said:

'The weather looks a little more settled.'

The other replied: 'I think it does.'

I bent my head and tapped the toe of my shoe with my stick, wishing to speak, wishing to go, but aware of a strong unknown power which made speech impossible and yet was not violent enough to detach me altogether and at once from the man standing there. Again my gaze wandered dallying to the hills—to the sky and the increase of stars—the darkness of the next hedge—the rushy green, the pale roads and the faint thicket mist that was starred with glow-worms. The scent of the honeysuckles and all those hedges was in the moist air. Now and then a few unexpected, startled and startling words were spoken, and the

silence drank them up as the sea drinks a few tears. But always my roving eyes returned from the sky, the hills, the plain to those other
greenish eyes in the dusk, and then with a growing sense of rest and
love to the copse waiting there, its indefinite cloud of leaves and
branches and, above that, the outline of oak tops against the sky. It was
very near. It was still, sombre, silent. It was vague and unfamiliar. I had
forgotten that it was a copse and one that I had often seen before.
White roses like mouths penetrated the mass of the hedge.

I found myself saying 'goodbye'. I heard the word 'goodbye' spoken.
It was a signal not of a parting but of a uniting. In spite of the un-
willingness to be silent with my friend a moment before, a deep ease
and confidence was mine underneath that unrest. I took one or two
steps to the stile and, instead of crossing it I leaned upon the gate at one
side. The confidence and ease deepened and darkened as if I also were
like that still, sombre cloud that had been a copse, under the pale sky
that was light without shedding light. I did not disturb the dark rest
and beauty of the earth which had ceased to be ponderous, hard matter
and had become itself cloudy or, as it is when the mind thinks of it,
spiritual stuff, so that the glow-worms shone through it as stars through
clouds. I found myself running without weariness or heaviness of the
limbs through the soaked overhanging grass. I knew that I was more
than the something which had been looking out all that day upon the
visible earth and thinking and speaking and tasting friendship. Somewhere—close at hand in that rosy thicket or far off beyond the ribs of
sunset—I was gathered up with an immortal company, where I and
poet and lover and flower and cloud and star were equals, as all the
little leaves were equal ruffling before the gusts, or sleeping and carved
out of the silentness. And in that company I had learned that I am something which no fortune can touch, whether I be soon to die or long
years away. Things will happen which will trample and pierce, but I
shall go on, something that is here and there like the wind, something
unconquerable, something not to be separated from the dark earth and
the light sky, a strong citizen of infinity and eternity. The confidence
and ease had become a deep joy; I knew that I could not do without the
Infinite, nor the Infinite without me.

Light and Twilight

The Path

Running along a bank, a parapet
That saves from the precipitous wood below
The level road, there is a path. It serves
Children for looking down the long smooth steep,
Between the legs of beech and yew, to where
A fallen tree checks the sight: while men and
        women
Content themselves with the road and what they see
Over the bank, and what the children tell.
The path, winding like silver, trickles on,
Bordered and even invaded by thinnest moss
That tries to cover roots and crumbling chalk
With gold, olive, and emerald, but in vain.
The children wear it. They have flattened the bank
On top, and silvered it between the moss
With the current of their feet, year after year.
But the road is houseless, and leads not to school.
To see a child is rare there, and the eye
Has but the road, the wood that overhangs
And underyawns it, and the path that looks
As if it led on to some legendary
Or fancied place where men have wished to go
And stay; till, sudden, it ends where the wood ends.

Collected Poems

Oxford Footpaths

The Oxford country is rich in footpaths, as any one will know that goes
the round from Folly Bridge, through South Hinksey, to the 'Fox' at
Boar's Hill (where the scent of wallflower and hawthorn comes in
through the window with the sound of the rain and the nightingale);
and then away, skirting Wootton and Cumnor, past the 'Bear' (with
its cool flagged room looking on a field of gold, and Cumnor Church

tower among elms); and back over the Hurst, where he turns, under
the seven firs and solitary elm, to ponder the long, alluring view towards Stanton Harcourt and Bablock Hythe. He may take that walk
many times, or wish to take it, and yet never touch the same footpaths; and never be sure of the waste patch of bluebell and furze,
haunted by linnet and whinchat; the newly harrowed field, where the
stones shine like ivory after rain; the green lane, where the beech leaves
lie in February, and rise out of the snow, untouched by it, in polished
amber; the orchard, where the grass is gloomy in April with the
shadow of bright cherry flowers.

One such footpath I remember, that could be seen falling among
woods and rising over hills, faint and winding, and disappearing at
last—like a vision of the perfect quiet life. We started once along it, over
one of the many fair little Oxford bridges, one that cleared the stream
in three graceful leaps of arching stone. The hills were cloudy with
woods in the heat. On either hand, at long distances apart, lay little
grey houses under scalloped capes of thatch, and here and there white
houses, like children of that sweet land—*albi circum ubera nati.* For the
most part we saw only the great hawthorn hedge, which gave us the
sense of a companion always abreast of us, yet always cool and fresh as
if just setting out. It was cooler when a red-hot bicyclist passed by. A
sombre river, noiselessly sauntering seaward, far away dropped with a
murmur, among leaves, into a pool. That sound alone made tremble
the glassy dome of silence that extended miles on miles. All things were
lightly powdered with gold, by a lustre that seemed to have been sifted
through gauze. The hazy sky, striving to be blue, was reflected as purple in the waters. There, too, sunken and motionless, lay amber willow
leaves; some floated down. Between the sailing leaves, against the false
sky, hung the willow shadows—shadows of willows overhead, with
waving foliage, like the train of a bird of paradise. Everywhere the
languid perfumes of corruption. Brown leaves laid their fingers on the
cheek as they fell; and here and there the hoary reverse of a willow leaf
gleamed in the crannied bases of the trees. A plough, planted in mid-
field, was curved like the wings of a bird alighting.

We could not walk as slowly as the river flowed; yet that seemed
the true pace to move in life, and so reach the great grey sea. Hand in
hand with the river wound the path, until twilight began to drive her
dusky flocks across the west, and a light wind knitted the aspen
branches against a silver sky with a crescent moon, as, troubled ten-

derly by autumnal maladies of soul, we came to our place of rest—a grey, immemorial house with innumerable windows.

Oxford

Women He Liked

Women he liked, did shovel-bearded Bob,
Old Farmer Hayward of the Heath, but he
Loved horses. He himself was like a cob,
And leather-coloured. Also he loved a tree.

For the life in them he loved most living things,
But a tree chiefly. All along the lane
He planted elms where now the stormcock sings
That travellers hear from the slow-climbing train.

Till then the track had never had a name
For all its thicket and the nightingales
That should have earned it. No one was to blame.
To name a thing beloved man sometimes fails.

Many years since, Bob Hayward died, and now
None passes there because the mist and the rain
Out of the elms have turned the lane to slough
And gloom, the name alone survives, Bob's Lane.

Collected Poems

The Icknield Way

At Swindon the explorer of the Icknield Way has all the world before him. He may go through Marlborough into the Pewsey Valley, and either along under the hills through Lavington to Westbury, or, turning out of the Pewsey Valley, to Old Sarum, and beyond Westbury or Sarum into the extreme west; and he will be on a road of the same type as the Icknield Way for the greater part of the distance. Or he may content himself with reaching Avebury. Or he may miss Avebury and aim at Bath. At present documents and traditions keep a perfect silence west of Wanborough, and among mere possibilities the choice is endless. The easiest, the pleasantest, and the wrongest thing to do is to take to the Ridgeway at Wanborough and follow it along the supposed south-westerly course under Liddington Hill, under Barbury Castle, and then up on to the ridge to Avebury. But though it is possible that in the Middle Ages this was done, there is little doubt that the green way going high up on the ridge past Glory Ann Barn is not coeval with, is not the same road as, the hill-foot road that has crept persistently but humbly under the Chilterns and Berkshire Downs. Such a road ran more risks than the Ridgeway from the plough. Its preservation between Upton and Lockinge Park is miraculous. It might easily have disappeared in the ploughland about Chiseldon or the rich pastures of Coate. Let the conjecturer thus skip a few miles in his westerly or south-westerly course, and he can go rapidly ahead, following under the main ridge to Avebury, or under the secondary ridge, three or four miles north of it, towards Calne and Bath. It is a game of skill which deserves a select reputation—to find an ancient road of the same character as the Oxfordshire and Berkshire Icknield Way, going west or south-west beyond Wanborough. The utmost reward of this conjecturing traveller would be to find himself on the banks of the Towy or beside the tomb of Giraldus at St. David's itself.

The Icknield Way

Entering Wales

The best way into Wales is the way you choose, provided that you care. Some may like the sudden modern way of going to sleep at London in a train and remaining asleep on a mountain-side, which has the advantage of being the most expensive and the least surprising way. Some may like to go softly into the land along the Severn, on foot, and going through sheath after sheath of the country, to reach at last the heart of it at peaty Tregaron, or the soul of it on Plynlimmon itself. Or you may go by train at night; and at dawn, on foot, follow a little stream at its own pace and live its fortnight's life from mountain to sea.

Or you may cross the Severn and then the lower Wye, and taking Tredegar and Caerleon alternately, or Rhigws and Landore, or Cardiff and Lantwit, or the Rhondda Valley and the Vale of Neath, and thus sharpening the spirit, as an epicure may sharpen his palate, by opposites, find true Wales everywhere, whether the rivers be ochre and purple with corruption, or still as silver as the fountain dew on the mountain's beard; whether the complexions of the people be pure as those of the young cockle-women of Penclawdd, or as heavily super-scribed as those of tin-platers preparing to wash. Or you may get no harm by treading in the footsteps of that warm-blooded antiquarian, Pennant, who wrote at the beginning of his tours in Wales: 'With obdurate valour we sustained our independency . . . against the power of a kingdom more than twelve times larger than Wales: and at length had the glory of falling, when a divided country, beneath the arms of the most wise and most warlike of the English monarchs.' That 'we' may have saved the soul even of an antiquarian.

But the entry I best remember and most love was made by a child whom I used to know better than I have known anyone else. He dis-appeared, after a slow process of evanishment, several years ago: and I will use what I know as if it were my own, since the first person singular will help me to write as if I should never be subjected to the dignity of print—as if I were addressing, not the general reader, but some one who cared.

At a very early age, I (that is to say, he *bien entendu*) often sat in a room in outer London, where I now see that it was probably good to be. It was always October there, and the yellow poplar leaves were always falling. And so also there was always a fire—a casket in which emeralds and sapphires contended with darker spirits continually. Where are the poplars now? Where the leaves which loved the frost that spoiled them at last? Where the emeralds and sapphires—and the child? There were late October twilights that seemed so mighty in their gentleness and so terrible in their silence that they alarmed the child with fear of desolation, until the spell was suspended by lighted lamps and drawn curtains and fearless voices of elder persons, though one could draw the curtains and see the thing still, and oneself, and the very fire, outside in its embrace. And still

The jealous ear of night eave-dropped our talk.

I think those twilights have overwhelmed all at last, and they have their way with child and trees and fire. But they have spared one thing, which even in those days was more puissant than the fire, though they have left their marks upon it, and now it seems a less mighty thing if one goes to it soberly, too critically, or even too cheerfully. For a picture hung in the room, and the last October sunlight used to fall upon it when the silence set in. The picture meant Wales.

In the foreground, a stream shone with ripples in the midst, and glowed with foam among the roots of alders at the edge. Branches with white berries overhung the stream; and there were hornbeams and writhen oaks; and beyond them, a sky with a shaggy and ancient storm in it, and wrestling with that, and rising into it, the ruins of an Early English chancel. The strength and anger and tenderness and majesty of it were one great thought. I still think that could deeds spring panoplied from thoughts, and could great thoughts of themselves do anything but flush the cheek, such a simply curving landscape as this would be at the bidding of one of those great thoughts that empty all the brain. . . . Under one of the columns by the chancel, the artist meant to have drawn vaguely a pile of masonry and a muscular ivy stem. And that was the point of the picture, because it seemed to be a kneeling knight . . . soon after I had become certain that the painter had somehow caught Launcelot kneeling at the foot of the column, I reached Wales.

There I saw one of the Round Tables of Arthur, but also a porpoise hunt in the river close by; and the porpoise threshed the water so that the shining spray now hides the Round Table from my view. And I heard the national anthem of Wales: and at first I cowered beneath the dresolved an terrible despair of it, forgetting that—

In every dirge there sleeps a battle-march;

so that I seemed to look out from the folds of a fantastic purple curtain of heavily embroidered fabric upon a fair landscape and an awful sky; and I know not whether the landscape or the sky was the more fascinating in its mournfulness.

And I heard sounds of insult, shame, and wrong,
And trumpets blown for wars—

and it was of Arthur's last battle that I dreamed. But the sky cleared, and I seemed to let go of the folds of the curtain and to see a red dragon triumphing and the shielded Sir Launcelot again; and next, it was only a tournament that I saw, and there were careless ladies on high among

the golden dust. And, at last, I could once more think happily of the
little white house where I lived, and the largest and reddest apples in all
the world that grew upon the wizened orchard, and the smoked
salmon and the hams that perfumed the long kitchen, and all the
shining candlesticks, and the wavy, crisp, thin leaves of oaten bread
that were eaten there with buttermilk: and the great fire shook his
rustling sheaf of flames and laughed at the wind and rain that stung the
window-panes; and sometimes a sense of triumph arose from the glory
of the fire and the vanity of the wind, and sometimes a sense of fear
lest the fire should be conspiring with the storm. That also was Wales—
a meandering village street, the house with the orchard, and a white
river in sight of it, and the great music of the national anthem hovering
over it and giving the whole a strange solemnity.

Just beyond the village, but not under the same solemn sky, I see
an island of apple trees in spring, which in fact belongs to a somewhat
later year. It was reached by a mile of winding lane that passed the
slender outmost branches of the village, and lastly, a shining cottage,
with streaked and mossy thatch, and two little six-paned windows,
half-filled with many-coloured sweets, and boasting one pane of bottle-
glass. Outside sat an old woman; her moist, grey, hempen curls
framing a cruel face which had been made by three or four swift
strokes of a hatchet; her magnificent brown eyes seeming to ponder
heavenly things and really looking for half-pence. A picture would have
made her—wringing her hands slowly as if she were perpetually washing, or sitting bolt upright and pleased with her white apron—a type
of resigned and reverend and beautiful old age. On the opposite side of
the road was a white and thatched piggery, half the size of the house;
and alongside of it, a neat, moulded pile of coal-dust, clay, and lime,
mixed, for her ever-burning fire. The pigs grunted; the old woman,
who would herself watch the slaughtering, sat and was pleased, and
said, 'Good morning', and 'Good afternoon', and 'Good evening' as
the day went by, except when the children were due to pass to and from
school, with half-pence to spend.

Just beyond this dragon and its house, an important road crossed the
lane, which then narrowed and allowed the hedgerow hazels to arch
over it and let in only the wannest light to the steep, stony hedge-bank
of whin and grass and fern and violets. Little streams ran this way and
that, under and over and alongside the lane, and at length a larger one
was honoured by a bridge, the parapet covered with flat, dense, even

turf. The bridge made way for a wide view, and to invite the eye a magpie flew away from the grassy parapet with wavy flight to a mountain side.

Between the bridge and the mountain, and in fact surrounded by streams which were heard although unseen, was an island of apple trees.

There were murmurs of bees. There was a gush and fall and gurgle of streams, which could be traced by their bowing irises. There was a poignant glow and fragrance of flowers in an air so moist and cold and still that at dawn the earliest bee left a thin line of scent upon it. Beyond, the mountain, grim, without trees, lofty and dark, was clearly upholding the low blue sky full of slow clouds of the colour of the mountain lambs or of melting snow. This mountain and this sky, for that first hour, shut out, and not only shut out but destroyed, and not only destroyed but made as if it had never been, the world of the old woman, the coal-pits, the schools, and the grown-up persons. And the magic of Wales, or of Spring, or of childhood made the island of apple trees more than an orchard in flower. For as some women seem at first to be but rich eyes in a mist of complexion and sweet voice, so the orchard was but an invisible soul playing with scent and colour as symbols. Nor did this wonder vanish when I walked among the trees and looked up at the blossoms in the sky. For in that island of apple trees there was not one tree but was curved and jagged and twisted and splintered by great age, by the west wind, or by the weight of fruit in many autumns. In colour they were stony. They were scarred with knots like mouths. Some of their branches were bent sharply like lightning flashes. Some rose up like bony, sunburnt, imprecating arms of furious prophets. One stiff, gaunt bole that was half hid in flower might have been Ares' sword in the hands of the Cupids. Others were like ribs of submerged ships, or the horns of an ox emerging from a skeleton deep in the sand of a lonely coast. And the blossom of them all was the same, so that they seemed to be Winter with the frail Spring in his arms. Nor was I surprised when the first cuckoo sang therein, since the blossom made it for its need. And when a curlew called from the mountain hopelessly, I laughed at it.

Wales

A Fellow Walker

When I sat down at the 'Dolau Cothi Arms' this evening I remembered my dedication to you. You said I could dedicate this book to you if I would make a real dedication, not one of my shadowy salutes befitting shadows rather than men and women. It seems odd you should ask thus for a sovereign's worth of—shall I say?—English prose from a writer by trade. But though I turn out a large, if insufficient, number of sovereigns' worths, and am become a writing animal, and could write something or other about a broomstick, I do not write with ease: so let that difficulty give the dedication its value.

It is right that I should remember you upon a walk, for I have walked more miles with you than with anyone else except myself. While I walked you very often danced, on the roads of Kent, Sussex, Surrey, and Hampshire. This evening when I went out on the Sarn Helen everybody was in chapel, I think, unless it was the Lord, for he also seemed to me to be walking in the cool. I was very much alone, and glad to be. You were a ghost, and not a man of fourteen stone, and I thought that perhaps after all that shadowy salute would be fittest. But I have put my pen to paper: I have set out and I will come to an end; for, as I said, I am a writing animal. In the days of those old walks I could have written a dedication in Norfolk-jacket style, all about 'the open road', and the search for something 'over the hills and far away': I should have reminded you at some length how Borrow stayed at this inn, and that Dolau Cothi is the house where he could have lived with satisfaction 'if backed by a couple of thousands a year.' Today I know there is nothing beyond the farthest of far ridges except a sign-post to unknown places. The end is in the means—in the sight of that beautiful long straight line of the Downs in which a curve is latent—in the houses we shall never enter, with their dark secret windows and quiet hearth smoke, or their ruins friendly only to elders and nettles— in the people passing whom we shall never know though we may love them. Today I know that I walk because it is necessary to do so in order both to live and to make a living. Once those walks might have made

a book; now they make a smile or a sigh, and I am glad they are in
ghostland and not fettered in useless print. This book for you was to
have been a country book, but I see that it has turned out to be another
of those books made out of books founded on other books. Being but
half mine it can only be half yours, and I owe you an apology as well
as a dedication. It is, however, in some ways a fitting book for me to
write. For it is about a road which begins many miles before I could
come on its traces and ends miles beyond where I had to stop. I could
find no excuse for supposing it to go to Wales and following it there
into the Ceidrych Valley, along the Towy to Caermarthen, and so to
St. David's which is now as holy as Rome, though once only a third
as holy. Apparently no special mediaeval use revived it throughout its
course, or gave it a new entity like that of the Pilgrims' Way from
Winchester to Canterbury that you and I walked on many a time—by
the 'Cock' at Detling, the 'Black Horse' at Thurnham, the 'King's
Head' (once, I believe, the 'Pilgrims' Rest') at Hollingbourne, above
Harrietsham, past Deodara Villas, above Lenham and Robert Philpot's
'Woodman's Arms', and so on to Eastwell; always among beech and
yew and Canterbury bells, and always over the silver of whitebeam
leaves. I could not find a beginning or an end of the Icknield Way. It is
thus a symbol of mortal things with their beginnings and ends always
in immortal darkness. I wish the book had a little more of the mystery
of the road about it. You at least will make allowances—and additions;
and God send me many other readers like you. And as this is the bottom
of the sheet, and ale is better than ink, though it is no substitute, I label
this 'Dedication', and wish you with me inside the 'Dolau Cothi Arms'
at Pumpsaint, in Caermarthenshire.

Dedication of *The Icknield Way* to Harry Hooton

THE LIE
OF THE LAND

Our Country

I had never before been in that lane of larches. It was, in fact, the first time that I had got out of London into pure country on foot. I had been by train to seaside resorts and the country homes of relatives, but this was different. I had no idea that London died in this way into the wild.

Out on the broad pasture bounded by a copse like a dark wall, rooks cawed in the oak-trees. Moorhens hooted on a hidden water behind the larches. At the end of a row of cottages and gardens full of the darkest dahlias was a small, grey inn called 'The George', which my companion entered. He came out again in a minute with bread and cheese for two, and eating slowly but with large mouthfuls we strolled on, too busy and too idle to talk. Instead of larches horse-chestnuts overhung our road; in the glittering grass borders the dark fruit and the white pods lay bright. So as we ate we stooped continually for the biggest 'conquers' to fill our pockets. Suddenly the other boy, musing and not looking at me, asked, 'What's your name?' 'Arthur Froxfield', I answered, pleased and not at all surprised. 'It doesn't suit you,' he said, looking at me. 'It ought to be John something—

"John, John, John,
With the big boots on."

You're tired.'

I knew his name well enough, for at twelve he was the best runner in the school. Philip Morgan. . . . I do not suppose that I concealed my pride to be thus in his company.

For an hour we were separated; we hit upon the trail, and off he went without a word. At a limping trot I followed, but lost sight of Philip and soon fell back into a walk. I had, in fact, turned homewards when he overtook me; he had been forced to retrace his steps. I was by this time worn out, and should have given up but for my self-satisfaction at the long run and the pleasure of knowing that he did not mind my hanging on his arm as on we crawled. Thus at last after an age of sleepy fatigue I found myself at home. It had been arranged that on the next day I was to go round to Abercorran House.

Again and again, Philip and I revisited that lane of larches, the long water-side copse, the oak wood out in the midst of the fields, and all the hedges, to find moorhen's eggs, a golden-crested wren's, and a thousand treasures, and felicity itself. Philip had known this country for a year or more; now we always went together. I at least, for a long time, had a strong private belief that the place had been deserted, overlooked, forgotten, that it was known only to us. It was not like ordinary country. The sun there was peculiarly bright. There was something unusual in the green of its grass, in the caw of its rooks in April, in the singing of its missel-thrushes on the little round islands of wood upon the ploughland. When later on I read about those 'remote and holy isles' where the three sons of Ulysses and Circe ruled over the glorious Tyrrhenians, I thought, for some reason or another, or perhaps for no reason, of those little round islands of ash and hazel amidst the ploughland of Our Country, when I was ten and Philip twelve. If we left it unvisited for some weeks it used to appear to our imaginations extraordinary in its beauty, and though we might be forming plans to go thither again before long, I did not fully believe that it existed—at least for others—while I was away from it. I have never seen thrushes' eggs of a blue equalling those we found there.

No wonder Our Country was supernaturally beautiful. It had London for a foil and background; what is more, on that first day it wore an uncommon autumnal splendour, so that I cannot hope to meet again such heavily gilded elms smouldering in warm, windless sunshine, nor such bright meadows as they stood in, nor such blue sky and such white billowy cloud as rose up behind the oaks on its horizon.

Philip knew this Our Country in and out, and though his opinion was that it was not a patch on the country about his old home at Abercorran, he was never tired of it. In the first place he had been introduced to it by Mr. Stodham. 'Mr. Stodham,' said Philip, 'knows more about England than the men who write the geography books. He knows High Bower, where we lived for a year. He is a nice man. He has a horrible wife. He is in an office somewhere, and she spends his money on jewellery. But he does not mind; remember that. He has written a poem and father does not want him to recite it. Glory be to Mr. Stodham. When he trespasses they don't say anything, or if they do it is only, "Fine day, sir," or "Where did you want to go to, sir," or "Excuse me, sir, I don't mind your being on my ground, but thought you mightn't be aware it is private." But if they catch you or me, especially you, being only eleven and peagreen at that, we shall catch it.'

Once he was caught. He was in a little copse that was all black-thorns, and the blackthorns were all spikes. Inside was Philip looking for what he could find; outside, and keeping watch, sat I; and it was Sunday. Sunday was the only day when you ever saw anyone in Our Country. Presently a man who was passing said: 'The farmer's coming along this road, if that's any interest to you.' It was too late. There he was—coming round the bend a quarter of a mile off, on a white pony. I whistled to Philip to look out. I was innocently sitting in the same place when the farmer rode up. He asked me at once the name of the boy in the copse, which so took me by surprise that I blabbed out at once. 'Philip Morgan,' shouted the farmer, 'Philip Morgan, come out of that copse.' But Philip was already out of it, as I guessed presently when I saw a labourer running towards the far end, evidently in pursuit. The farmer rode on, and thinking he had given it up I followed him. However, five minutes later Philip ran into his arms at a gateway, just as he was certain he had escaped, because his pursuer had been out-classed and had given up running. In a few minutes I joined them. Philip was recovering his breath and at the same time giving his address. If we sent in five shillings to a certain hospital in his name, said the farmer, he would not prosecute us—'No,' he added, 'ten shillings, as it is Sunday.' 'The better the day the better the deed,' said Philip scornfully. 'Thank you, my lad,' said the giver of charity, and so we parted. But neither did we pay the money, nor were we prosecuted: for my father wrote a letter from his official address. I do not know what he said. In future, naturally, we gave some of our time and trouble to avoiding the white pony when we were in those parts. Not that he got on our nerves. We had no nerves. No: but we made a difference. Besides, his ground was really not in what we called Our Country, *par excellence*. Our own country was so free from molestation that I thought of it instantly when Aurelius read to me about the Palace of the Mountain of Clouds. A great king had asked his coun-sellors and his companions if they knew of any place that no one could invade, no one, either man or genie. They told him of the Palace of the Mountain of Clouds. It had been built by a genie who had fled from Solomon in rebellion. There he had dwelt until the end of his days.

After him no one inhabited it; for it was separated by great distances and great enchantment from the rest of the world. No one went thither. It was surrounded by running water sweeter than honey, colder than snow, and by fruitful trees. And there in the Palace of the Mountain of Clouds the king might dwell in safety and solitude for ever and ever. . . .

In the middle of the oak wood we felt as safe and solitary as if we were lords of the Palace of the Mountain of Clouds. And so we were. For four years we lived charmed lives. For example, when we had manufactured a gun and bought a pistol, we crawled over the ploughed fields at twilight, and fired both at a flock of pewits. Yet neither birds nor poachers suffered. We climbed the trees for the nests of crows, woodpeckers, owls, wood-pigeons, and once for a kestrel's, as if they were all ours. We went everywhere. More than once we found ourselves among the lawns and shrubberies of big houses which we had never suspected. This seems generally to have happened at twilight. As we never saw the same house twice the mysteriousness was increased. One of the houses was a perfect type of the dark ancient house in a forest. We came suddenly stumbling upon it among the oaks just before night. The walls were high and craggy, and without lights anywhere. A yew tree grew right up against it. A crow uttered a curse from the oak wood. And that house I have never seen again save in memory. There it remains, as English as Morland, as extravagantly wild as Salvator Rosa. That evening Philip must needs twang his crossbow at the crow—an impossible shot; but by the grace of God no one came out of the house, and at this distance of time it is hard to believe that men and women were actually living there.

Most of these estates had a pond or two, and one had a long one like a section of a canal. Here we fished with impunity and an untroubled heart, hoping for a carp, now and then catching a tench. But often we did not trouble to go so far afield. Our own neighbourhood was by no means unproductive, and the only part of it which was sacred was the Wilderness. None of the birds of the Wilderness ever suffered at our hands. Without thinking about it we refrained from fishing in the Wilderness pond, and I never saw anybody else do so except Higgs, but though it seemed to me like robbing the offertory Higgs only grinned. But other people's grounds were honoured in a different way. Private shrubberies became romantic at night to the trespasser. Danger doubled their shadows, and creeping amongst them we missed no ecstasy of which we were capable. The danger caused no conscious anxiety or fear, yet contrived to heighten the colour of such expeditions. We never had the least expectation of being caught. Otherwise we should have had more than a little fear in the January night when we went out after birds, armed with nets and lanterns. The scene was a region of meadows, waiting to be built on and in the meantime occupied by a few horses and cows, and a football and a lawn-tennis club. Up and down the hedges we went with great hopes of four and twenty blackbirds or so. We had attained a deep and thrilling satisfaction but not taken a single bird when we were suddenly aware of a deep, genial voice asking, 'What's the game?' It was a policeman. The sight acted like the pulling of a trigger—off we sped. Having an advantage of position I was the first to leap the boundary hedge into the road, or rather into the ditch between hedge and road. Philip followed, but not the policeman. We both fell at the jump, Philip landing on top of me, but without damage to either. We reached home, covered in mud and secret glory, which made up for the loss of a cap and two lanterns. The glory lasted one day only, for on the next I was compelled to accompany my father to the police-station to inquire after the cap and lanterns. However, I had the honour of hearing the policeman say—though laughing—that we had taken the leap like hunters and given him no chance at all. This and the fact that our property was not recovered preserved a little of the glory.

In these meadows, in the grounds which their owners never used at night, and in Our Country, Philip and I spent really a great deal of time, fishing, birds-nesting, and trying to shoot birds with cross-bow, pistol, or home-made gun. There were intervals of school, and of football and cricket, but these in memory do not amount to more than the towns of England do in comparison with the country. As on the map the towns are but blots and spots on the country, so the school-hours were embedded, almost buried away, in the holidays, official, semi-official, and altogether unofficial. Philip and I were together during most of them; even the three principal long holidays of the year were often shared, either in Wales with some of Philip's people, or at Lydiard Constantine, in Wiltshire, with my aunt Rachel.

The Happy-Go-Lucky Morgans

Salisbury Plain

Before the first brightening of the light on Sunday morning the rain ceased, and I returned to Dunbridge to pick up the road I had lost on Saturday evening. Above all, I wanted to ride along under Dean Hill, the level-ridged chalk hill dotted with yew that is seen running parallel to the railway a quarter of a mile on your left as you near Salisbury from Eastleigh. The sky was pale, scarcely more blue than the clouds with which it was here and there lightly whitewashed. For five miles I was riding against the stream of the river which rises near Clarendon and meets the Test near Dunbridge. The water and its alders, many of them prostrate, and its drab sedges mingled with intense green and with marsh-marigolds' yellow, were seldom more than a hundred yards away on my right. Pewits wheeled over it with creaking wings and protests against the existence of man.

I did not stop for the villages. Butts Green, for example, where the Other Man had seen the fox weather-vane, began with an old thatched cottage and a big hollow yew, but the green itself was dull, flat, and bare, and the cottages round it newish. Lockerley Green, a mile farther on, was much like it, except that the road traversed instead of skirting the green. Between these two, and beyond Lockerley Church, where the road touched the river and had a fork leading across to East Tytherley, there was a small, but not old, mill, and a miller too, and flour. As I looked back, the small sharp spire of the church stuck up over the level ridgy ploughland in a manner which, I supposed, would have made for a religious person a very religious picture. No other building was visible. The railway on my left was more silent than the river on my right, among its willow and alder and tall, tufted grass, at the foot of gorse slopes.

After crossing the railway half a mile past Lockerley Green the road went close to the base of Dean Hill, separated from it by ploughland without a hedge. On the left, that is on the Dean Hill side, stood East Dean Church, a little rustic building of patched brick and plaster walls, mossy roof, and small lead-paned windows displaying the Easter decorations of moss and daffodils. It had a tiny bell turret at the west end, and a round window cut up into radiating panes like a geometrical spider's web. Under the yew tree, amidst long grass, dandelion, and celandine, lay the bones of people bearing the names Edney and Langridge. The door was locked. Its neighbours on the other side of the road were an old cottage with tiled roof and walls of herring-boned brick, smothered from chimney to earth with ivy, in a garden of plum blossom; and next to it, a decent, small home, a smooth clipped block of yew, and a whitewashed mud wall with a thatched coping. The other houses of East Dean, either thatched or roofed with orange tiles, were scattered chiefly on the right.

Presently I had the willows of the river as near me on the right as the green slope, the chalk pit, the sheep-folds, and yew trees of Dean Hill on the left; and the sun shone upon the water and began to slant down the hillside. The river was very clear and swift, the chalk of its bed very white, the hair of its waving weeds very dark green.

West Dean, where I entered Wiltshire, a mile from East Dean, is a village with a 'Red Lion' inn, a railway station, a sawmill and timber-yard, and several groups of houses clustering close to both banks of the river, which is crossed by a road-bridge and by a white footbridge below. I went over river and railway uphill past the new but ivied church to look at the old farm-house, the old church, and the camp, which lie back from the road on the left among oaks and thickets. On that Sunday morning cows pasturing on the rushy fields below the camp, and thrushes singing in the oaks, were the principal inhabitants of West Dean. I did not go farther in this direction, for the road went north to West Tytherley and the broad woods that lie east of it, the remnant of Buckholt Forest, but turned back and west, and then south-west again on my original road, in order to be on the road nearest to Dean Hill. This took me over broad and almost hedgeless fields, and through a short disconnected fragment of an avenue of mossy-rooted beeches, to West Dean Farm. Nothing lay between the houseless road and the hillside, which is thick here with yew, except the broad arable fields, with a square or two given up to mustard flowers and sheep, and West Dean Farm itself. It is a house of a dirty white colour amidst numerous and roomy outbuildings, thatched or mellow-tiled, set in a circle of tall beeches. The road bends round the farm group and goes straight to the foot of the hill, and then along it. I went slowly, looking up at the yews and thorns on the green wall of the hill, and its slanting

green trackway, and the fir trees upon the ridge. Linnets twittered in
companies or sang solitarily on thorn tips. Thrushes sang in the wayside
yews. Larks rose and fell unceasingly. The sheep-bells tinkled in the
mustard. Away from the hill the land sloped gradually in immense
arable fields, and immense grass fields newly rolled into pale green
stripes, down to the river, and there rose again up to Hound Wood and
Bentley Wood, where a white house shone pale in the north-east, four
or five miles off.

For nearly two miles the road had not had a house upon it, and
nothing separated me from the hill, the yew trees, and the brier and
hawthorn thickets. In fact, West Dean Farm was the only house
served by the three miles of road between West Dean and West Grimstead. Yet this did not save a chalk pit close to the road from being used
as a receptacle for rubbish. Having reached the farm and the foot of the
hill the road began to turn away again towards the river and to West
Grimstead. It was a loose, flinty road, so that I had another reason for
walking instead of riding. The larks that sang over me could not have
wished for better dust baths than this road would make them, for the
sun was gaining. It was almost a treeless road until I was close to West
Grimstead, where there was an oak wood on the right, streaked with
the silver of birch stems and tipped with the yellow flames of larches.
The village consisted of a church, an inn called the 'Spring Cottage',
and many thatched cottages scattered along several by-roads on either
side. It ended in an old thatched cottage with outbuildings, at the verge
of a deep sand pit full of sand-martins' holes. When I had passed it I
stopped at a gate and looked at the orange pit wall on the far side, the
cottage above the wall, and the elm between the road and the pit. A
thrush and several larks were singing, and through their songs I heard
a thin voice that I had not heard for six months, very faint yet unmistakable, though I could not at once see the bird—a sand-martin. I
recognized the sound, as I always recognize at their first autumnal
ascent above the horizon the dim small cluster of the Pleiades on a
September evening. On such a morning one sand-martin seems enough
to make a summer, and here were six, flitting in narrow circles like
butterflies with birds' voices.

I went on and found myself in a flat land of oak woods and of fields
that were half molehills and half rushes, and the hedge banks had gorse
in blossom. It was here that I joined the Southampton and Salisbury
road, a yellow road between the gorsy, rolling fragments of Whaddon

Common, which came to an end at a plantation of pines on and about some mounds like tumuli on the right hand.

Uphill to Alderbury I walked, looking back south-eastward along the four-mile wall of Dean Hill which I had quitted a mile behind. Alderbury, its 'Green Dragon', its public seat and foursquare fountain of good water for man and beast (erected by Jacob, sixth Earl of Radnor), is on a hilltop overlooking the Avon, and immediately on leaving it I began to descend and to slant nearer and nearer the river. The hedges of the road guided my eyes straight to the cathedral spire of Salisbury, two or three miles off beneath me. On the right the sward and oaks of Ivychurch came down to the road: below on the left the sward was wider, the oaks were fewer, and many cows were feeding. A long cleft of rushy turf and oaks, then a broad ploughland succeeded the Ivychurch oaks, and the ploughland rose up into a round summit crested by a clump of pines and beeches. I remember seeing this field when it was being ploughed by two horses, and the ploughman's white dog was exploring on one side or another across the slopes.

Over beyond the river the land swelled up into chalk hills, here smooth and green, with a clump on the ridge, and there wooded. The railway was now approaching the road from the right, and the narrow strip between road and railway was occupied by an old orchard and a large green chestnut tree. In the branches of the chestnut sang a chaffinch, while a boy was trimming swedes underneath. I was now at the suburban edge of Salisbury, the villas looking out of their trees and lemon-coloured barberry at the double stream of Avon, at the willowy marshland, the cathedral, and the Harnham Down racecourse above.

I crossed over Harnham bridge where the tiled roofs are so mossy, and went up under that bank of sombre-shimmering ivy just to look from where the roads branch to Downston, Blandford, and Odstock. Southward nothing is to be seen except the workhouse and the many miles of bare down and sheepfolds. Northward the cathedral spire soars out of a city without a hill, dominated on the right or east by Burroughs Hill, a low but decided bluff, behind which are the broad woods of Clarendon. The road was deserted. It was on a Tuesday evening, after market, that I had last been there, when clergy with wives and daughters were cycling out past a wagon for Downton drawn by horses with red and blue plumelets; motor cyclists were tearing in; a tramp or two trudged down towards the bridge. In the city itself the cattle were being driven to the slaughter-house or out to the country, a spotted calf was prancing on the pavement, one was departing for Wilton in a crowded motor bus, a wet, new-born one stood in a cart with its mother, a cow with udders wagging was being hustled up the Exeter road by motor cars and pursued at a distance by a man who called to it affectionately as a last resource; another calf was being held outside a pub, while the farmer drank; black and white pigs were steered cautiously past plate glass; and in the market-place Sidney Herbert and Henry Fawcett on their pedestals were looking out over the dark, wet square at the last drovers and men in gaiters leaving it, and ordinary passengers crossing it, and a few sheep still bleating in a pen. And the green river meadows and their elms and willows chilled and darkened as the gold sun sank without staining the high, pale-washed sky, and the cathedral clock nervously and quietly said, 'One-two, one-two, one-two' for the third quarter before dark.

But this was Sunday morning, and still early. I ate breakfast to the tune of the 'Marseillaise', sung slowly and softly to a child as a lullaby, and was soon out again, this time amidst jackdaws, rooks, clergy, and the black-dressed Sunday procession, diversified by women in violet, green, and curry colour. The streets, being shuttered and curtained, robbed of the crowd shopping, were cold and naked; even the inns of Salisbury, whose names are so genial and succulent—'Haunch of Venison', 'Round of Beef', 'Ox', 'Royal George', 'Roebuck', 'Wool Pack'—were as near as possible dismal. Their names were as meaningless as those of the dead Browns, Dowdings, Burtons, Burdens, and Fullfords in St. Edmund's Churchyard. If it had not been for the women it would have been a city of the dead or a city of birds. The people kept to the paths of the close. The lawns and trees were given over exclusively to the birds, especially those that are black, such as the rook and blackbird. Those that were not matrimonially engaged on the grass were cawing in the elms, beeches, and chestnuts of the cathedral. Missel-thrushes were singing across the close as if it had been empty. A lark from the fields without drifted singing over the city. The stock-doves cooed among the carved saints. There were more birds than men in Salisbury. Never had I seen the cathedral more beautiful. The simple form of the whole must have been struck out of glaucous rock at one divine stroke. It seemed to belong to the birds that flew about it and lodged so naturally in the high places. The men who crawled in at the doors, as into mines, could not be the masters of such a vision.

Nevertheless, I took the liberty of entering myself, chiefly to look again for those figures of Death and a Traveller, where the Traveller says—

> *Alas, Death, alas, a blissful thing that were*
> *If thou wouldst spare us in our lustiness*
> *And come to wretches that be so of heavy cheer. . . .*

and Death retorts—

> *Graceless gallant, in all thy lust and pride,*
> *Remember that thou shalt give due,*
> *Death shall from thy body thy soul divide.*
> *Thou must not him escape certainly.*
> *To the dead bodies cast down thine eye,*
> *Behold them well, consider and see,*
> *For such as they are such shalt thou be.*

There is little more to be said about death than is said here. But I could not find the words, though I went up and down those streets of knights', ladies', and doctors' tombs, and saw again old Eleonor Sadler, grim, black, and religious, kneeling at her book in a niche since 1622, and looking as if she could have been the devil to those who did not do likewise. I saw, too, the tablet of Henry Hele, who practised medicine felicitously and honourably, for fifty years, in the close and in the city; and the green lady with the draped harp mourning over Thomas, Baron Wyndham, Lord High Steward of Ireland (1681–1745), and the bust of Richard Jefferies—

> *Who, observing the works of Almighty God*
> *With a poet's eye, | Has |*
> *enriched the literature of his country, | and |*
> *won for himself a place amongst | those |*
> *who have made men happier, | and wiser.*

If Jefferies had to be commemorated in a cathedral, it was un-necessary to drag in Almighty God. Perhaps the commemorator hoped thus to cast a halo over the man and his books; but I think 'The Story of my Heart' and 'Hours of Spring' will be proof against the holy water of these feeble and ill divided words.

In Pursuit of Spring

The Country of Richard Jefferies

Richard Jefferies was born at Coate Farm, in the North Wiltshire hamlet of Coate and the parish of Chisledon, on 6th November 1848. There he dwelt for the greater part of the first thirty years of his life; there and thereabouts, and in the neighbouring county of Gloucestershire, dwelt his ancestors for several, perhaps many, generations. This country and its people was the subject of half his work, and the background, the source, or the inspiration, of all but all the rest. He, in his turn, was the genius, the human expression, of this country, emerging from it, not to be detached from it any more than the curves of some statues from their maternal stone. He walked about the hills and fields of it day and night, in pursuit of sport, of health, of society, of solitude, of joy, of the dearest objects of his soul; and though he left it never to return, yet three times before he died he lived in, or in sight of, country not unlike it—at Brighton, at Crowborough, and at Goring.

It is a beautiful, a quiet, an unrenowned, and a most visibly ancient land. The core and essence of it are the Downs, which lie south and east and west of Coate. Northward is Swindon, where Jefferies lived two years, and Wootton Bassett, Purton, Malmesbury, Cirencester, and Fairford—all of which he knew, with their surrounding fields; but to reach them was to leave the Downs for the rich, sluggish, dairy country of elms, that is seldom roused to the energy of hills. Fair as that part of Wiltshire is, it has left few marks upon his books; and even in his youthful chapters on the Swindon neighbourhood, where he might have thought it his business to set his affection aside, he seldom betrays much knowledge of the northward land, of whose people Aubrey wrote that they 'speak drawling', are 'dull and heavy of spirits', 'feed chiefly on milk meats, which hurts their inventions', are 'melancholy, contemplative, malicious, by consequence whereof come more lawsuits—at least double those in the southern parts', and are 'more apt to be fanatic'. Roughly speaking, the Wiltshire and Berkshire Canal, in its course from near Wantage, past Uffington, Stratton St. Margaret, Swindon, Wootton Bassett, and Dauntsey, was Jefferies' northern boundary. That boundary at least in winter he loved, for the frosts turned it into an incomparable track for his skates, and it is as a skater only that he is respectfully remembered in those parts. The canal has now relapsed into barbarism; its stiffened and weedy waters are stirred only by the moorhen, who walks more than she swims across them.

For Jefferies at Coate, the summer sun rose over Whitehorse Hill, eight miles off in Berkshire, with the ancient entrenchment above and the westward-ramping, white horse below; and to reach the hill meant a long, lonely walk on the Ridgeway through the high corn-land and past Wayland Smith's cave, or along the more frequented parallel road below, through Wanborough, Little Hinton, Bishopston, Ashbury, and Compton Beauchamp. At Bishopston stood the old mansion— used as a Grammar School—which he has celebrated in 'Wild Life in a Southern County', in 'An Extinct Race', and in his early chapter on the London and Faringdon road. At Hinton and Bishopston there are fine farmhouses with lime trees; at Ashbury, also, one among trees and oats, built of stone, with many square windows and handsome chimneys; and one where the by-road goes to Longcott and Shrivenham. North of this road is the flat land, which has so many elms bordering so many small fields that from a distance it seems one wood. South, and close at hand, are the Downs—the solitary, arable slopes, the solid beech-clumps, the coursing and racing turf of Ashdown and Lambourn. Always high up, the Ridgeway goes north-eastward over the corn, with few traces of living men except the Oxford Steam-Ploughing Company's engines, harboured, perchance, amidst heaps of coal and the chalkland flowers—hop-trefoil, saw-wort, scabious, purple gentian, and poppy. Wayland Smith's cave lies on the left going north-east, about thirty water-worn and mossy sarsens, some roughly hewn, three upright, with a superincumbent fourth, hidden among beeches and starved elders. Beyond, the old road is to be seen going rough and white up Whitehorse Hill, nicked by the entrenchment, and with it even the weary feet must go if it is summer and the hour a spacious and windless twilight. It leads to yet another camp, Letcombe Castle, two or three miles south of Wantage, farther than which a walker from Coate who had to return the same day would not be likely to travel.

Going south-east instead of north-east from Coate, a similar limit is reached at Lambourn. From Wanborough, through Totterdown, to Baydon, the road is the Ermine Street on its way to Cirencester, through Cricklade, to Speen, and crosses the Ridgeway at Totterdown. For the ear at least Baydon is Badon Mount. This is pure down-land: the breasted hills curving as if under the influence of a great melody; the beeches lining the Roman road, and sheltering a gipsy camp among harebells, sweet basil, and trefoil, which the grasshopper also loves. Lambourn itself is a fair, small town, with a cross, of which the shaft is as graceful and light as the beeches in the churchyard. It is the hub of many little roads that lead out among the curving expanses of pasture and corn-land; the tumuli, in one place seven together, give a solemn tone to so much sweetness and space. Between Baydon and Aldbourne, and about Sugar Hill, the country is more park-like. There is a green and hedgeless turf, with knots and trains of beeches and thorns, and many little undulations and barbaric, winding tracks, startled and sundered by the straight Roman road. Thence the eyes enjoy Martinsell Hill, gentle and large, above standing and reaped corn and the trees of Aldbourne. The road from Baydon to Aldbourne is notable for its passage through one of the finest hollows in the Downs. The unbroken undulations are long, and the mind floats with them and sleeps in the melody which they make: there is grass, mangolds, wheat in leaning shocks, solid beech clusters, and, far away, on the edge of the bowl, Liddington clump; nor is there a house visible among the trackways, the haystacks, the sheep, and the corn, this side of the embowered Aldbourne church tower.

The Life of Richard Jefferies

Downland

Beyond the gateway the Downland and the corn begins, and with it the rain, so that the great yellow-banded bee hangs long pensive on the lilac flower of the scabious. Hereby is a farm with a wise look in its narrow window on either side of the white door under the porch; the walls of the garden and the farmyard are topped with thatch; opposite rises up a medlar tree, russet-fruited: and those two eyes of the little farm peep out at the stranger. From the next hill-top the land spreads out suddenly—an immense grey hedgeless land of pasture and ploughland and stubble with broadcast shadows of clouds and lines, and clumps of dark-blue trees a league apart. These woods are of pine and thorn and elder and beam, and some yew and juniper, haunted by the hare and the kestrel, by white butterflies going in and out, by the dandelion's down. Sometimes under the pines a tumulus whispers a gentle *siste viator* and the robin sings beside. Far away, white rounds of cloud bursting with sunlight are lifted up out of the ground; born of earth they pause a little upon the ridge and then take flight into the blue profound, their trains of shadow moving over the corn sheaves, over the ploughs working, along brown bands of soil, the furzy spaces, the deeply cloven grassy undulations, the lines of yews and of cornstacks. Slowly a spire like a lance-head is thrust up through the Downs into the sky.

Beyond the spire a huge woody mound rises up from the low flowing land, huge and carved all round by an entrenchment as if by the weight of a crown that it had worn for ages. Certainly it wears no crown today. Not a human being lives there; they have all fled to the riverside and the spire, leaving their ancient home to the triumphs of the wide-flowering traveller's joy, to the play of children on the sward within its walls, and to the archaeologist: and very sad and very noble it looks at night when it and the surrounding Downs lift up their dark domes of wood among the mountains of the sky, and the great silence hammers upon the ears.

Then a hedgeless road traverses without interrupting the long Downs. One after another, lines of trees thin and dark and old come out against the pale bright sky of late afternoon and file away, beyond the green turf and roots and the grey or yellow stubble. As the sun sets, dull crimson, at the foot of a muslin of grey and gold which his course has crimsoned, the low clouds on the horizon in the north become a deathly blue white belonging neither to day nor to night, while overhead the light-combed cloudlets are touched faintly with flame. Now the glory and the power of the colour in the west, and now the pallid north, fill the brain to overflowing with the mingling of distance, of sublime motion, and of hue, and intoxicate it and give it wings, until at last when the west is crossed by long sloping strata as of lava long cooled they seem the bars of a cage impassable. But even they are at last worn away and the sky is as nothing compared with earth. For there, as I move, the infinite greys and yellows of the crops, the grass, the bare earth, the clumps of firs, the lines of beeches and oaks, play together in the twilight, and the hills meet and lose their lines and flow into one another and build up beautiful lines anew, the outward and

visible signs of a great thought. Out of the darkness in which they are
submerged starts a crying of pewits and partridges; and overhead and
close together the wild duck fly west into the cold gilded blue.

The South Country

Over the Hills

Often and often it came back again
To mind, the day I passed the horizon ridge
To a new country, the path I had to find
By half-gaps that were stiles once in the hedge,
The pack of scarlet clouds running across
The harvest evening that seemed endless then
And after, and the inn where all were kind,
All were strangers. I did not know my loss
Till one day twelve months later suddenly
I leaned upon my spade and saw it all,
Though far beyond the sky-line. It became
Almost a habit through the year for me
To lean and see it and think to do the same
Again for two days and a night. Recall
Was vain: no more could the restless brook
Ever turn back and climb the waterfall
To the lake that rests and stirs not in its nook,
As in the hollow of the collar-bone
Under the mountain's head of rush and stone.

Collected Poems

Lakes and Pools

And of lakes, I have known Llyn-y-Fan Fach, the lonely, deep, gentle
lake on the Caermarthen Fan, two thousand feet high, where, if the
dawn would but last a few moments longer, or could one swim but
just once more across, or sink but a little lower in its loving icy depths,

one would have such dreams that the legend of the shepherd and the
lady whom he loved and gained and lost upon the edge of it would
fade away: and Llyn Llech Owen, and have wondered that only one
legend should be remembered of those that have been born of all the
gloom and the golden lilies and the plover that glories in its loneliness;
for I stand in need of a legend when I come down to it through rolling
heathery land, through bogs, among blanched and lichened crags, and
the deep sea of heather, with a few flowers and many withered ones, of
red and purple whin, of gorse and gorse-flower, and (amongst the
gorse) a grey curling dead grass, which all together make the desolate
colour of a 'black mountain'; and when I see the water for ever waved
except among the weeds in the centre, and see the water-lily leaves
lifted and resembling a flock of wild-fowl, I cannot always be content
to see it so remote, so entirely inhuman, and like a thing a poet might
make to show a fool what solitude was, and as it remains with its one
poor legend of a man who watered his horse at a well, and forgot to
cover it with the stone, and riding away, saw the water swelling over
the land from the well, and galloped back to stop it, and saw the lake
thus created and bounded by the track of his horse's hooves; and thus
it is a thing from the beginning of the world that has never exchanged
a word with men, and now never will, since we have forgotten the
language, though on some days the lake seems not to have forgotten it.
And I have known the sombre Cenfig water among the sands, where I
found the wild goose feather with which I write.

And I have seen other waters; but least of them all can I forget the
little unnecessary pool that waited alongside a quiet road and near a
grim, black village. Reed and rush and moss guarded one side of it,
near the road; a few hazels overhung the other side; and in their dis-
contented writhing roots there was always an empty moorhen's nest,
and sometimes I heard the bird hoot unseen (a sound by which the pool
complained, as clearly as the uprooted trees over the grave of Poly-
dorus complained), and sometimes in the unkind grey haze of winter
dawns, I saw her swimming as if vainly she would disentangle herself
from the two golden chains of ripples behind her. In the summer, the
surface was a lawn of duckweed on which the gloom from the hazels
found something to please itself with, in a slow meditative way, by
showing how green could grow from a pure emerald, at the edge of
the shadow, into a brooding vapourish hue in the last recesses of the
hazels. The smell of it made one shudder at it, as at poison. An artist

would hardly dare to sit near enough to mark all the greens, like a family of snaky essences, from the ancient and mysterious one within to the happy one in the sun. When the duckweed had dissolved in December, the pool did but whisper that of all things in that season, when

Blue is the mist and hollow the corn parsnep,

it alone rejoiced. It was in sight of the smoke and the toy-like chimney-stacks of the village, of new houses all around, and of the mountains. It had no possible use—nothing would drink of it. It did not serve as a sink, like the blithe stream below. It produced neither a legend nor a brook. It was a whole half-acre given up to a moorhen and innumerable frogs. It was not even beautiful. And yet, there was the divinity of the place, embodied, though there was no need for that, in the few broken brown reeds that stood all the winter, each like a capital Greek *lambda*, out of the water. When the pool harboured the image of the moon for an hour in a winter night, it seemed to be comforted. But when the image had gone, the loss of that lovely captive was more eloquent than the little romantic hour. And I think that, after all, the pool means the beauty of a pure negation, the sweetness of utter and resolved despair, the greatness of Death itself.

Wales

The Ash Grove

Half of the grove stood dead, and those that yet lived made
Little more than the dead ones made of shade.
If they led to a house, long before they had seen its fall:
But they welcomed me; I was glad without cause and delayed.

Scarce a hundred paces under the trees was the interval—
Paces each sweeter than sweetest miles—but nothing at all,
Not even the spirits of memory and fear with restless wing,
Could climb down in to molest me over the wall

That I passed through at either end without noticing.
And now an ash grove far from those hills can bring

The same tranquillity in which I wander a ghost
With a ghostly gladness, as if I heard a girl sing

The song of the Ash Grove soft as love uncrossed,
And then in a crowd or in distance it were lost,
But the moment unveiled something unwilling to die
And I had what most I desired, without search or desert or cost.

Collected Poems

An Old Wood

The chestnut blossom is raining steadily and noiselessly down upon a path whose naked pebbles receive mosaic of emerald light from the interlacing boughs. At intervals, once or twice an hour, the wings of a lonely swallow pass that way, when alone the shower stirs from its perpendicular fall. Cool and moist, the perfumed air flows, without lifting the most nervous leaf or letting fall a suspended bead of the night's rain from a honeysuckle bud. In an indefinite sky of grey, through which one ponderous cloud billows into sight and is lost again, no sun shines: yet there is light—I know not whence; for the brass trappings of the horses beam so as to be extinguished in their own fire. There is no song in wood or sky. Some one of summer's wandering voices—bullfinch or willow wren—might be singing, but unheard, at least unrealized. From the dead-nettle spires, with dull green leaves stained by purple and becoming more and more purple towards the crest, which is of a sombre uniform purple, to the elms reposing at the horizon, all things have bowed the head, hushed, settled into a perfect sleep. Those elms are just visible, no more. The path has no sooner emerged from one shade than another succeeds, and so, on and on, the eye wins no broad dominion.

It is a land that uses a soft compulsion upon the passer-by, a compulsion to meditation, which is necessary before he is attached to a scene rather featureless, to a land that hence owes much of its power to a mood of generous reverie which it bestows. And yet it is a land that gives much. Companionable it is, reassuring to the solitary; he soon has a feeling of ease and seclusion there. The cool-leaved wood!

The limitless, unoccupied fields of marsh marigold, seen through the trees, most beautiful when the evening rain falls slowly, dimming and almost putting out the lustrous bloom! Gold of the minute willows underfoot! Leagues of lonely grass where the slow herds tread the daisies and spare them yet!

Towards night, under the sweet rain, at this warm, skyless close of the day, the trees, far off in an indolent, rolling landscape, stand as if disengaged from the world, in a reticent and pensive repose.

But suddenly the rain has ceased. In an old, dense wood the last horizontal beams of the sun embrace the trunks of the trees and they glow red under their moist ceiling of green. A stile to be crossed at its edge, where a little stream, unseen, sways the stiff exuberant angelica that grows from it, gives the word to pause, and with a rush the silence and the solitude fill the brain. The wood is of uncounted age; the ground on which it stands is more ancient than the surrounding fields, for it rises and falls stormily, with huge boulders here and there; not a path intrudes upon it; the undergrowth is impenetrable to all but fox and bird and this cool red light about the trunks of the trees. Far away a gate is loudly shut, and the rich blue evening comes on and severs me irrevocably from all but the light in the old wood and the ghostly white cow-parsley flowers suspended on unseen stalks. And there, among the trees and their shadows, not understood, speaking a forgotten tongue, old dreads and formless awes and fascinations discover themselves and address the comfortable soul, troubling it, recalling to it unremembered years not so long past but that in the end it settles down into a gloomy tranquillity and satisfied discontent, as when we see the place where we were unhappy as children once. Druid and devilish deity and lean wild beast, harmless now, are revolving many memories with me under the strange, sudden red light in the old wood, and not more remote is the league-deep emerald sea-cave from the storm above than I am from the world.

The Heart of England

It Rains

It rains, and nothing stirs within the fence
Anywhere through the orchard's untrodden, dense

Forest of parsley. The great diamonds
Of rain on the grassblades there is none to break,
Or the fallen petals further down to shake.

And I am nearly as happy as possible
To search the wilderness in vain though well,
To think of two walking, kissing there,
Drenched, yet forgetting the kisses of the rain:
Sad, too, to think that never, never again,

Unless alone, so happy shall I walk
In the rain. When I turn away, on its fine stalk
Twilight has fined to naught, the parsley flower
Figures, suspended still and ghostly white,
The past hovering as it revisits the light.

Collected Poems

Cornwall

In Cornwall, where the wrinkles and angles of the earth's age are left
to show, antiquity plays a giant's part on every hand. What a curious
effect have those ruins, all but invisible among the sands, the sea-blue
scabious, the tamarisk and rush, though at night they seem not inaudible when the wild air is full of crying! Some that are not nearly
as old are almost as magical. One there is that stands near a great
water, cut off from a little town and from the world by a round green
hill and touched by no road but only by a wandering path. At the foot
of this hill, among yellow mounds of sand, under blue sky, the church
is dark and alone. It is not very old—not five centuries—and is of
plainest masonry: its blunt short spire of slate slabs that leans slightly to
one side, with the smallest of perforated slate windows at the base, has
a look of age and rusticity. In the churchyard is a rough grey cross of
stone—a disk supported by a pillar. It is surrounded by the waving
noiseless tamarisk. It looks northward over the sandhills at a blue bay,
guarded on the west by tall grey cliffs which a white column sur-
mounts.

For a time the nearer sandhills have rested and clothed themselves in bird's-foot trefoil, thyme, eyebright and short turf: but once the church was buried beneath them. Between the round hill and the church a tiny stream sidles along through a level hiding-place of flags and yellow flag flowers, of purple figwort and purple orchis and green grass.

A cormorant flies low across the sky—that sable bird which seems to belong to the old time, the time of badger and beaver, of ancient men who rose up out of the crags of this coast. To them, when the cuckoo first called one April, came over the blue sea a small brown ship, followed by three seals, and out of it descended a Christian from Ireland, black-haired, blue-eyed, with ready red lips and deep sweet voice and spoke to them, all alone. He told them of a power that ruled the blue waters and shifting sands, who could move the round green hill to the rock of the white gulls; taller and grimmer than the cloven headland yet sweet and gentle as the fennel above; deep-voiced as the Atlantic storm, tender also as the sedge-warbler in the flags below the hill; whose palace was loftier than the blue to which the lark was now soaring, milder and richer than the meadows in May and everlasting; and his attendants were more numerous and bright than the herring under a moon of frost. The milk-pails should be fuller and the grass deeper and the corn heavier in the ear if they believed in this; the pilchards should be as water boiling in the bay; and they should have wings as of the white birds that lounged about the precipices of the coast. And all the time the three seals lay with their heads and backs above the shallows and watched. Perhaps the men believed his word; perhaps they dropped him over the precipice to see whether he also flew like a gull: but here is the church named after him.

All along the coast (and especially where it is lofty and houseless, and on the ledges of the crags the young grey gulls, unable to fly, bob their heads seaward and try to scream like their parents who wheel far and near with double yodelling cry), there are many rounded barrows looking out to sea. And there are some amidst the sandhills, bare and corrugated by the wind and heaved up like a feather-bed, their edges golden against the blue sky or mangily covered by drab marram grass that whistles wintrily; and near by the blue sea, slightly roughened as by a harrow, sleeps calm but foamy among cinder-coloured isles; donkeys graze on the brown turf, larks rise and fall and curlews go by; a cuckoo sings among the deserted mines. But the barrows are most noble on the high heather and grass. The lonely turf is full of lilac

scabious flowers and crimson knapweed among the solid mounds of
gorse. The brown-green-grey of the dry summer grass reveals myriads
of the flowers of thyme, of stonecrop yellow and white, of pearly
eyebright, of golden lady's fingers, and the white or grey clover with
its purest and earthiest of all fragrances. Here and there steep tracks
descend slantwise among the thrift-grown crags to the sea, or promise
to descend but end abruptly in precipices. On the barrows themselves,
which are either isolated or in a group of two or three, grow thistle and
gorse. They command mile upon mile of cliff and sea. In their sight the
great headlands run out to sea and sinking seem to rise again a few miles
out in a sheer island, so that they resemble couchant beasts with backs
under water but heads and haunches upreared. The cliffs are cleft many
times by steep-sided coves, some with broad sand and shallow water
among purple rocks, the outlet of a rivulet; others ending precipitously so that the stream suddenly plunges into the black sea among
a huddle of sunless boulders. Near such a stream there will be a grey
farm amid grey outbuildings—with a carved wooden eagle from the
wreckage of the cove, or a mermaid, once a figure-head with fair long
hair and round bosom, built into the wall of a barn. Or there is a
briny hamlet grouped steeply on either side of the stream which
gurgles among the pebbles down to the feet of the bearded fisherman
and the ships a-gleam. Or perhaps there is no stream at all, and bramble
and gorse come down dry and hot to the lips of the emerald and
purple pools. Deep roads from the sea to the cliff-top have been worn
by smuggler and fisherman and miner, climbing and descending. Inland shows a solitary pinnacled church tower, rosy in the warm
evening—a thin line of trees, long bare stems and dark foliage matted—
and farther still the ridges of misty granite, rough as the back of a perch.

Of all the rocky land, of the sapphire sea white with quiet foam, the
barrows are masters. The breaking away of the rock has brought them
nearer to the sea as it has annihilated some and cut off the cliff-ways in
mid-career. They stand in the unenclosed waste and are removed from
all human uses and from most wayfaring. Thus they share the sub-
limity of beacons and are about to show that tombs also have their
deaths. Linnet and stonechat and pipit seem to attend upon them, with
pretty voices and motions and a certain ghastliness, as of shadows, given
to their cheerful and sudden flittings by the solemn neighbourhood.
But most of their hold upon the spirit they owe to their powerful
suggestion that here upon the high sea border was once lived a bold

c

proud life, like that of Beowulf, whose words, when he was dying from the wounds of his last victory, were: 'Bid the warriors raise a funeral mound to flash with fire on a promontory above the sea, that it may stand high and be a memorial by which my people shall remember me, and seafarers driving their tall ships through the mist of the sea shall say: "Beowulf's Mound". '

In Cornwall as in Wales, these monuments are the more impressive, because the earth, wasting with them and showing her bones, takes their part. There are days when the age of the Downs, strewn with tumuli and the remnants of camp and village, is incredible; or rather they seem in the course of long time to have grown smooth and soft and kind, and to be, like a rounded languid cloud, an expression of Earth's summer bliss of afternoon. But granite and slate and sandstone jut out, and in whatsoever weather speak rather of the cold, drear, hard, windy dawn. Nothing can soften the lines of Trendreen or Brown Willy or Carn Galver against the sky. The small stone-hedged plough-lands amidst brake and gorse do but accentuate the wildness of the land from which they have been won. The deserted mines are frozen cries of despair as if they had perished in conflict with the waste; and in a few years their chimneys standing amidst rotted woodwork, the falling masonry, the engine rusty, huge and still (the abode of rabbits, and all overgrown with bedstraw, the stern thistle and wizard henbane) are in keeping with the miles of barren land, littered with rough silvered stones among heather and furze, whose many barrows are deep in fern and bramble and foxglove. The cotton grass raises its pure nodding white. The old roads dive among still more furze and bracken and bramble and foxglove, and on every side the land grows no such crop as that of grey stones. Even in the midst of occasional cornfield or weedless pasture a long grey upright stone speaks of the past. In many places men have set up these stones, roughly squaring some of them, in the form of a circle or in groups of circles—and over them beats the buzzard in slow hesitating and swerving flight. In one place the work of Nature might be mistaken for that of man. On a natural hillock stands what appears to be the ruin of an irregularly heaped wall of grey rock, roughened by dark-grey lichen, built of enormous angular fragments like the masonry of a giant's child. Near at hand, bracken, pink stonecrop, heather and bright gold tormentil soften it; but at a distance it stands black against the summer sky, touched with the pathos of man's handiwork overthrown, yet certainly an accident of

Nature. It commands Cape Cornwall and the harsh sea, and St. Just with its horned church tower. On every hand lie cromlech, camp, circle, hut and tumulus of the unwritten years. They are confused and mingled with the natural litter of a barren land. It is a silent Bedlam of history, a senseless cemetery or museum, amidst which we walk as animals must do when they see those valleys full of skeletons where their kind are said to go punctually to die. There are enough of the dead; they outnumber the living; and there those trite truths burst with life and drum upon the tympanum with ambiguous fatal voices. At the end of this many-barrowed moor, yet not in it, there is a solitary circle of grey stones, where the cry of the past is less vociferous, less bewildering, than on the moor itself, but more intense. Nineteen tall, grey stones stand round a taller, pointed one that is heavily bowed, amidst long grass and bracken and furze. A track passes close by, but does not enter the circle; the grass is unbent except by the weight of its bloom. It bears a name that connects it with the assembling and rivalry of the bards of Britain. Here, under the sky, they met, leaning upon the stones, tall, fair men of peace, but half-warriors, whose songs could change ploughshare into sword. Here they met, and the growth of the grass, the perfection of the stones (except that one stoops as with age), and the silence, suggests that since the last bard left it, in robe of blue or white or green—the colours of sky and cloud and grass upon this fair day—the circle has been unmolested, and the law obeyed which forbade any but a bard to enter it. Sky-blue was the colour of a chief bard's robe, emblematic of peace and heavenly calm, and of unchangeableness. White, the colour of the Druid's dress, was the emblem of light, and of its correlatives, purity of conduct, wisdom, and piety. Green was the colour of the youthful ovate's robe, for it was the emblem of growth. Their uniformity of colour signified perfect truth. And the inscription upon the chair of the bards of Beisgawen was, 'Nothing is that is not for ever and ever.' Blue and white and green, peace and light and growth—'Nothing is that is not for ever and ever'—these things and the blue sky, the white, cloudy hall of the sun, and the green bough and grass, hallowed the ancient stones, and clearer than any vision of tall bards in the morning of the world was the tranquil delight of being thus 'teased out of time' in the presence of this ancientness.

The South Country

The Combe

The Combe was ever dark, ancient and dark.
Its mouth is stopped with bramble, thorn, and briar;
And no one scrambles over the sliding chalk
By beech and yew and perishing juniper
Down the half precipices of its sides, with roots
And rabbit holes for steps. The sun of Winter,
The moon of Summer, and all the singing birds
Except the missel-thrush that loves juniper,
Are quite shut out. But far more ancient and dark
The Combe looks since they killed the badger there,
Dug him out and gave him to the hounds,
That most ancient Briton of English beasts.

Collected Poems

Poppies

The earliest mower had not risen yet; the only sign of human life was
the light that burned all night in a cottage bedroom, here and there;
and from garden to garden went the white owl with that indolent
flight which seems ever about to cease, and he seemed to be the dis-
embodied soul of a sleeper, vague, homeless, wandering, softly taking
a dim joy in all the misty, dense forget-me-not, pansy, cornflower,
Jacob's ladder, wallflower, love-in-a-mist, and rose of the borders,
before the day of work once more began.

So I followed the owl across the green and past the church until I
came to the deserted farm. There the high-porched barn, the doorless
stables, the cumbered stalls, the decaying house, received something of
life from the owl, from the kind twilight, or from my working mind.
Above the little belfry on the housetop the flying fox of the weather

vane was still, fixed for ever by old age in the south, recording not the hateful east, the crude and violent north, the rainy west wind. Whether because the buildings bore upon their surfaces the marks of many generations of life, all harmoniously continuous, or whether because though dead and useless they yet seemed to enjoy and could speak to a human spirit, I do not know, but I could fancy that, unaided, they were capable of inspiring afresh the idea of immortality to one who desired it. Mosses grew on the old tiles and were like moles for softness and rotundity. A wind that elsewhere made no sound talked meditatively among the timbers. The village Maypole, transported there a generation ago, stood now as a flagstaff in the yard, and had it burst into leaf and flower it would hardly have surprised. Billows of tall, thick nettle, against the walls and in every corner, were a luxuriant emblem of all the old careless ease of the labourers who, despite their sweat and anxiety and hopelessness, yet had time to lean upon their plough or scythe or hoe to watch the hounds or a carriage go by. Tall tansy and fleabane and hawkweeds and dandelions, yellow blossoms, stood for the bright joys of the old life. The campions on the hedge, the fumitory in the kitchen garden, meant the vague moods between sorrow and joy, speaking of them as clearly as when from out of the church flows the litany, charged with the emotion of those who hear it not, though lying near. Had the wise owner admitted these things and for their sake obeyed the command of the will which bade him leave the Green Farm untouched? He might well have done so had he seen the birth of colour after colour in the dawn.

At first, when doves began to coo and late cuckoos to call in invisible woods beyond, I thought that the green of grass was alive again; but that was only because I knew it was grass and could translate its grey. The green trees were still black above a lake of white mist far off when the yellows of hawkweed and tansy rose up. The purple fumitory, the blue of speedwells, came later. And then, as I turned a shadowy corner and came out into the broad half-light just before sunrise, I saw the crimson of innumerable poppies that had a thought of mist pearl enmeshed amongst them.

They were not fifty yards away—they were in a well-known place—and yet there towered high walls and gloomed impassable moats between them and me, such was the strangeness of their beauty. Had they been reported to me from Italy or the East, had I read of them on a supreme poet's page, they could not have been more remote, more inaccessible, more desirable in their serenity. Something in me desired them, might even seem to have long ago possessed and lost them, but when thought followed vision as, alas! it did, I could not understand their importance, their distance from my mind, their desirableness, as of a far-away princess to a troubadour. They were stranger than the high stars, as beautiful as any woman new-born out of summer air, though I could have reaped them all in half an hour. A book in a foreign, unknown language which is known to be full of excellent things is a simple possession and untantalizing compared with these. They proposed impossible dreams of strength, health, wisdom, beauty, passion—could I but relate myself to them more closely than by won-der, as a child to a ship at sea which, after all, he may one day sail in, or of a lover for one whom he may some day attain. I was glad and yet I fatigued myself by a gladness so inhuman. Did men, I asked myself, once upon a time have simply an uplifting of the heart at a sight like this? Or were they destined in the end to come to that—a blissful end? Had I offended against the commonwealth of living things that I was not admitted as an equal to these flowers? Why could they not have vanished and left me with my first vision, instead of staying and repeat-ing that it would be as easy to draw near to the stars as to them?

And yet the mind is glad, if it is troubled, of an impossible, far-away princess. She deceives the mind as Columbus deceived his weary sailors by giving out at the end of each day fewer knots than they had truly travelled, in order that they should not lose courage at the immensity of the voyage.

And still the poppies shone and the blackbird sang from his tower of ivory.

The Heart of England

Surrey

Then I saw a huge silence of meadows, of woods, and beyond these, of hills that raised two breasts of empurpled turf into the sky; and, above the hills, one mountain of cloud that beamed as it reposed in the blue as in a sea. The white cloud buried London with a *requiescat in pace*.

I like to think how easily Nature will absorb London as she absorbed the mastodon, setting her spiders to spin the winding-sheet and her worms to fill in the graves, and her grass to cover it pitifully up, adding flowers—as an unknown hand added them to the grave of Nero. I like to see the preliminaries of this toil where Nature tries her hand at mossing the factory roof, rusting the deserted railway metals, sowing grass over the deserted platforms and flowers of rose-bay on ruinous hearths and walls. It is a real satisfaction to see the long narrowing wedge of irises that runs alongside and between the rails of the South-Eastern and Chatham Railway almost into the heart of London. And there are many kinds of weather when the air is full of voices prophesying desolation. The outer suburbs have almost a moorland fascination when fog lies thick and orange-coloured over their huge flat wastes of grass, expectant of the builder, but does not quite conceal the stark outlines of a traction engine, some procumbent timber, a bonfire and frantic figures darting about it, and aerial scaffolding far away. Other fields, yet unravished but menaced, the fog restores to a primeval state. And what a wild noise the wind makes in the telegraph wires as in wintry heather and gorse! When the waste open spaces give way to dense streets there is a common here and a lawn there, where the poplar leaves, if it be November, lie taintless on the grass, and the starlings talk sweet and shrill and cold in the branches, and nobody cares to deviate from the asphalt path to the dewy grass: the houses beyond the green mass themselves gigantic, remote, dim, and the pulse of London beats low and inaudible, as if she feared the irresistible enemy that is drawing its lines invisibly and silently about her on every side. If a breeze arises it makes that sound of the dry curled leaves chafing along the pavement; at night they seem spies in the unguarded by-ways. But there are also days—and spring and summer days, too—when a quiet horror thicks and stills the air outside London.

The South Country

Chalk Pits

It is sometimes consoling to remember how much of the pleasantness of English country is due to men, by chance or design. The sowing of various crops, the planting of hedges and building of walls, the trimming of woods to allow trees to grow large and shapely, and so on, are among the designed causes of this pleasantness. Here men have obviously co-operated with Nature. But as great effects are produced when they have seemed at first to insult or ignore her. A new house, for example, however well proportioned, and however wisely chosen the material, is always harsh to the eye and the mind. In a hundred years it little matters what the form or the material; if the house survives, and is inhabited for a century, it has probably made its place. If it is deserted, it makes a place yet more rapidly. There is no building which the country cannot digest and assimilate if left to itself in about twenty years. Cottage or factory or mansion is powerless against frost, wind, rain, grass and ivy, and the entirely assimilated building is always attractive unless the beholder happens to know the reason why it was deserted; and even if he does, his sympathy will very likely not conflict with his sense of beauty, but will aid it in secret—that is what is consoling. London deserted would become a much pleasanter place than Richard Jefferies pictured it in *After London*. The mere thought of the jackdaws who would dwell there is a cheerful one, and they would not be alone. I like to think what mysteries the shafts, the tubes, the tunnels and the vaults would make, and what a place to explore. The railway cuttings, unless very steep-sided, soon become romantic, and near London they are a refuge for many plants and insects.

But among the works of men that rapidly become works of Nature, and can be admired without misanthropy, are the chalk and marl pits. The great ones are pleasing many miles away, both in themselves and through association. On a hill-side they always assume a good shape, like those of a scallop shell or even of a fan. Those on the Downs above Lewes, Maidstone and Midhurst, will be remembered. Against their white walls we can like the limeworks themselves, whether they offer only the ordinary black chimneys as at Buriton, or whether they are majestic in their arched masonry like those which are consuming the Dinas above Llandebie in Carmarthenshire. If there were only one of these fans or scallops of white low down on a bare hill-side it would be as celebrated as the inverted fan of Fujiyama in Japan. They are impressive, I think, chiefly as being, with the exception of glass-houses and sheets of water, the only distinctly luminous objects on the comparatively dark earth. They show up like arched windows or doorways of gigantic proportions lighted from within the hills. Their all but perpendicular walls take long to be grassed over when deserted, even if the rabbits do not seek refuge in them and keep the chalk moving by their narrow terraces. Perhaps that enormous scoop is one that has been so grassed over, on the steep hill-side facing southward near East Meon. It is completely covered with fine grass, and has an almost level green floor, which is used as a playing field. It bears the name of 'The Vineyard', and it has been suggested that it was used by the Romans or Romanized Britons for the cultivation of vines. But this is very much like one of the lesser natural combes of the chalk country, and except for its name, and possible use, it has no particular interest. The lesser chalk pits are the better. These may be divided roughly into two kinds —first, those which are dug out of more or less level ground, and are shaped like a bowl or funnel, or a series of such; second, those which have been carved out of a slope. Those upon a slope are usually the more charming to the eye. They are met, for example, suddenly where the road bends round a steep bank, and whether the chalk is dazzling or shadowed it is welcome. The white or grey-white wall is overhung by roots of ash and beech trees, and if it be old by a curtain of traveller's joy or ivy. These overhanging roots and climbers often form a covered way large enough for a man to creep through, and much used by foxes and lesser beasts. At the foot is a waste space of turf. Here grows the wayfaring tree with its pendent clusters of cherry-coloured fruit, or the beam tree, whose leaves fall with their heavy sides uppermost and so lie all through the winter; or perhaps bracken and purple-stemmed angelica, nine feet high and straight, with graceful bracketed frondage all still; or perhaps the sweetest flowers of the chalk, the yellow St. John's wort, birdsfoot, agrimony, and hawkweed, the pink bramble and mallow, the mauve marjoram and basil, the purple knapweed, and to these come the Red Admiral and Peacock and Copper butterflies, the bright-winged flies and bees, and the grasshoppers like emerald armoured horsemen—four white butterflies float past hundreds of flowers without heeding them, and then all four try to alight on one. The air is full of the sweetness of wild carrot and parsnip seeds. Sometimes the floor is filled up with a dense Paradise of bramble and blackthorn, and there is a nightingale in it or a blackcap and in the winter a wren.

The hollow pits are not so familiar, because they lie often in the middle of the fields which they used to supply with chalk. They may be so shallow that they have been ploughed over, and now merely serve to break the surface of a great cornfield. Or they may be deep like mines, so that the chalk had to be raised by a windlass; and these are now protected by rails, and used only for depositing carrion. As a rule the bowl-shaped pits have been overgrown by bushes, or where large enough, planted with trees, with beech, oak, ash and holly; and they are surrounded by a hedge to keep out cattle. They have names of their own; often they are dells, such as Stubridge Dell, or Slade Dell. Thus they often form pretty little islands of copse in the midst of arable, and show their myriads of primroses or bluebells through the hazels when the neighbour field is crumbling dry in an east wind. These islands are attractive largely, I think, because they suggest fragments of primaeval forest that have been left untouched by the plough on account of their roughness. I call them islands because that is the impression made on the passer-by. Cross over to them, and they are seen to be more like ponds full of everything but water. There are some small ones brimful of purple rosebay flowers in the midst of the corn. Others are full of all that a goldfinch loves—teasel, musk, thistle and sunshine. One is so broken up by the uneven diggings, the roots of trees, and the riot of brambles that a badger is safe in it with a whole pack of children. Some farms have one little or big dell to almost every field, and to enter-prising children there must be large tracts of country which exist chiefly to provide these dells. One or two of the best of them are half-way between the hollow pit and the hill-side scoop. One in particular, a vast one, lies under a steep road which bends round it, and has to pro-tect its passengers by posts and rails above the perpendicular. At the upper side it is precipitous, but it has a level floor, and the old entrance below is by a very gradual descent. It is very old, and some of the trees, which are now only butts, must have been two centuries old when they were felled. It is big enough for the Romany Rye to have fought there with the Flaming Tinman. But in Borrow's days it had more trees in it. Now it has about a score of tall ash trees only, ivy covered, and almost branchless, rising up out of it above the level of the road. Except at midsummer, only the tops of the ash trees catch the sunlight. The rest is dark and wild, and somehow cruel. The woodmen looked tiny and dark, as if working for a punishment, when they were felling some of the trees below. That hundred yards or so of road running round the edge of the ancient pit is as fascinating as any other similar length in England. From the rails above you could well watch the Romany Rye and the Flaming Tinman and fair-haired Isopel. But except the woodmen and the horses drawing out the timber, no one visits it. It is too gloomy. This is no vineyard, unless for growing the ruby grape of Proserpine, the nightshade. Though roofed with the sky, it has the effect of a cave, an entrance to the underworld.

Other roadside dells, facing the south or southwest, are not so deserted. The old chalk pits, being too steep and rough to be cultivated, soon grow into places as wild as ancient Britain. They are especially good at a meeting of several roads. They form wayside wastes which are least easily enclosed. These strips are, or were, called slangs, and a waste of a larger kind gave us the curious word Flash. Flash is a village in a wild quarter of Derbyshire, between Buxton and Macclesfield. The people were mostly squatters who used the place as headquarters when they were not travelling to and from the fairs; and the lingo in which they talked to one another was called flash-talk. There is flash-talk still to be heard in some of the wayside chalk pits. There is no better place for a camp than one of these with a good aspect. It gives a man a little of the sense of a room. At the best it has almost four walls, which keep out neither sun nor rain. Some of them are much used by tramps and gipsies and other travellers, until they are enclosed on the ground that these persons are a nuisance or are spoiling the beauty of the country. I think these travellers ought to be protected—say by the Zoological Society. Many of them are happy and they are at least as interesting, though often not as beautiful, as anything at the Zoo. They cost very little, being far too meek to steal much. For the price of a first-rate cigar one of them could be fed for a week, or a family for a bottle of wine. They give endless quiet amusement to civilized men who here behold what they have come from and what some of them would like to return to again. It seems to requite some philosophy to sit high on the Downs on a rainy February day, reading half a sheet of a week-old daily paper, on the leeside of a copse which was once a chalk pit. I have seen the man several times, but never observed that anyone was sitting at his feet to learn his wisdom. He had not wife, nor other possessions, nor desire to converse. He was lean, dirty, quite unpicturesque and not strong, but he made the best of a wet February day. Most men would have preferred to be one of the chestnut horses ploughing near, their coats marked as with the hammer-marks on copper.

In summer, he and his kind are more picturesque. The best group I ever saw—and it was at the entrance to a chalk pit—was three wild women in black rags, with a perambulator and a large black cat. They had hair like hemp, and glittering blue eyes. They were lean but tall and strong. They were quite silent. When I first saw them they had a fire and were cooking—the cat knew what—upon a windy Sunday morning, while the church bells were ringing.

They were not supernatural, I can swear, because one of them asked the time as I left, though it was upon a solitary and remote roadway, and they appeared to have no affairs in this world that could depend upon 'the time'. I laughed at the question, and they seemed surprised, but they were too busy—thinking, shall I say?—to say any more. Two days later the races at——began, but they were not there. On the morning of the races human beings crawled out of all kinds of holes, and the chalk pits supplied one or two. There is, presumably, no horse-racing after death, so that the lot of these devotees is not to be envied, though in this world they seem content. I saw one crawl out of an archway where a considerable stream of water ran in winter. But the chalk pit was better—it seemed to hold, as in a treasury, half the sun of a glorious morning, and across the floor, beside a dead fire, sprawled a middle-aged sportswoman in old black velvet, fast asleep, though the race-goers were streaming past in some haste. Those were the days of the green-finches—little bands flitting and twittering through hedges and over yew trees with clear thin notes, breezy in the breeze—and of linnets scattering now over the brassy ragwort flowers, and millions of poppies in the wheat. Once I met a small bear in one of the tangled dells in this neighbourhood. He was curled up in the sun between bushes of gorse, and his master's head was buried in his fur. If the bear had been alone it might have been a scene in Britain before Caesar's time, but though it was 1904 the bear looked indigenous. This dell is one of those which may be natural or artificial, or perhaps partly both, a small natural combe having been convenient for excavation in the chalk. It lies at the foot of a wild Down which is climbed, chiefly for the sake of its chalk pits, by a slanting steep road. The dell is a long narrow chamber with a floor rising towards the beginning of the steep slope. The sides of it are worn by the rabbits and support little but gaunt elder bushes. The floor grows a few ash trees and much gorse. The tallest tree is dead, but the combe is sheltered and the great ash still holds up its many arms in the form of a lyre, high above the rest. It is grey and stiff and without bark. But the jackdaws love it. All through the afternoons of summer they come and go among the hills, and the dead tree is their chief station. It might almost seem a religious place to them. There are always two or three perched on the topmost branches, talking to those arriving or departing. Now and then a turtledove flies up and they do not resent it. As to the bear, it was nothing to them. Their ancestors had seen many such. There are jackdaws in the elms of the neighbouring meadows, but those religious ones upon the dead ash tree seem the most important, and it alone is never deserted.

The Last Sheaf

Sussex

A few miles south of that great presiding pollard beech is the boundary line between Surrey and Kent on the north and Sussex on the south. A few miles over the line the moorland organ roll of heather and birch and pine succeeds the grassy undulations and the well-grown beech and oak. The yellow roving lines of the paths cut through the heather into the sand add to the wildness of the waste, by their suggestion of mountain torrents and of channels worn in the soft rock or clay by the sea. The same likeness in little is often to be seen upon a high-pitched roof of thatch when the straw is earth-coloured and tunnelled by birds and seamed by rain. Here the houses are of stone, unadorned, heather-thatched. The maker of birch-heath brooms plies his trade. There are stacks of heath and gorse in the yard. All the more fair are the grooves in the moorland, below the region of pines, where the tiled white-boarded mill stands by the sheen of a ford, and the gorse is bright and white clothes are blowing over neat gardens and the first rose. On a day of rain and gloom the answer of the gorse to sudden lights and heats is delicious; all those dull grey and glaucous and brown dry spines bursting into cool and fragrant fire is as great a miracle as the turning of flames to roses round a martyr's feet.

It is only too easy for the pheasant lords to plant larch in parallelograms: to escape from them it is necessary to go in amongst them. Yet there are parts of the forest large and dark and primeval in look, with a few poor isolated houses and a thin file of telegraph posts crossing it among the high gloomy pines and down to the marshy hollows, to the strewn gold of dwarf willows, and up again to the deserted wooden windmill, the empty boarded cottage, the heather-thatched sheds at the southern edge of the moor. Looking at this tract of wild land the mind seems to shed many centuries of civilization and to taste something of the early man's alarm in the presence of the uncultured hills—an alarm which is in us tempered so as to aid an impression of the sublime. Its influence lingers in the small strips of roadside gorse beyond its proper boundary. Then, southward, there are softly dipping meadows, fields of young corn, and oaks thrown among the cowslips. The small farmhouses are neat and good—one has a long stone wall in front, and, over the road, tall Scotch firs above a green pond dappled by the water crowfoot's white blossoms and bordered by sallow and rush. Narrow copses of oak or wide hedges of hazel and sallow line the road; and they are making cask hoops under lodges of boughs at the woodsides. Bluebells and primroses and cuckoo flowers are not to be counted under the trees. The long moist meadows flow among the woods up and down from farm to farm and spire to tower. Each farm-house group is new—this one is roofed and walled with tiles; and opposite is a tangle of grass and gorse, with fowls and hen-coops amongst it, a sallowy pond, a pile of faggots, some crooked knees of oak, some fresh-peeled timber: old grey hop poles lean in a sheaf all round a great oak. The gates are of good unpainted oak, and some few are of a kind not often seen elsewhere, lower than a hurdle and composed of two stout parallel bars united by twenty uprights and by two pieces meeting to form a V across these. The gates deserve and would fill a book by themselves.

Green lucent calipers of flags shadow one another in little wayside ponds, white-railed; for this is the Weald, the land of small clay ponds. The hazels are the nightingale's. In many of the oak woods the timber carriages have carved a way through primroses and bluebells deep into the brown clay. The larger views are of cloudy oak woods, ridge behind ridge, and green corn or grass and grey ploughland between; and of the sun pouring a molten cataract out of dark machicolated clouds on to one green field that glows a moment and is insignificant again: the lesser are of little brambly precipitous sandpits by the road, of a white mill at a crossing, of carved yews before black-timbered inns, of a starling that has learned the curlew's call perched on a cottage roof, of abeles all rough silver with opening leaf shivering along the grass-bordered evening road, of two or three big oaks in a meadow corner and in their shadow unblemished parsley and grasses bowed as if rushing in the wind. At an inn door stands a young labourer, tall and straight but loosely made, his nose even and small, his eyes blue and deep set, his lips like those of Antinous, his face ruddy and rough-grained, his hair short and brown and crisp upon his fair round head;

his neck bound by a voluminous scarf (with alternate lozenges of crimson and deep green divided by white lines) that is gathered beneath his chin by a brass ring and thence flows down under his blue coat; his trousers of grey cord, dirty and patched with drab to a weathered stone colour, fitting almost tightly to his large thighs and calves and reaching not too near to his small but heavily-shod feet. A prince—a slave. He is twenty, unmarried, sober, honest, a noble animal. He goes into a cottage that stands worn and old and without a right angle in its timbers or its thatch any more than in its apple trees and solitary quince which all but hide the lilac and massed honesty of the little garden. This is a house—I had almost said this is a man—that looked upon England when it could move men to such songs as, 'Come, live with me and be my love', or—

> 'Hey, down a down!' did Dian sing,
> Amongst her virgins sitting;
> 'Than love there is no vainer thing,
> For maidens most unfitting.'
> And so think I, with a down, down derry.

For a moment or less as he goes under the porch I seem to see that England, that swan's nest, that island which a man's heart was not too big to love utterly. But now what with Great Britain, the British Empire, Britons, Britishers, and the English-speaking world, the choice offered to whomsoever would be patriotic is embarrassing, and he is fortunate who can find an ideal England of the past, the present, and the future to worship, and embody it in his native fields and waters or his garden, as in a graven image.

The round unending Downs are close ahead, and upon the nearest hill a windmill beside a huge scoop in the chalk, a troop of elms below, and then low-hedged fields of grass and wheat. The farms are those of the downland. One stands at the end of the elm troop that swerves and clusters about its tiled roof, grey cliff of chimney-stack, and many gables; the stables with newer tiles; the huge slope of the barn; the low mossy cart-lodge and its wheels and grounded shafts; the pale straw stacks and the dark hay ricks with leaning ladders. A hundred sheep-bells rush by with a music of the hills in the wind. The larks are singing as if they never could have done by nightfall. It is now the hour of sunset, and windy. All the sky is soft and dark-grey-clouded except where the sun, just visible and throbbing in its own light, looks through a bright window in the west with a glow. Exactly under the sun the grass and wheat is full both of the pure effulgence and of the south-west wind, rippling and glittering: there is no sun for anything else save the water. North of the sun and out of its power lies a lush meadow, beyond it a flat marshland cut by several curves of bright water, above that a dark church on a wooded mound, and then three shadowy swoops of Down ending at a spire among trees.

South-west, the jagged ridgy cluster of a hillside town, a mill and a castle, stand dark and lucid, and behind them the mere lines of still more distant downs.

The South Country

The Barn

They should never have built a barn there, at all—
Drip, drip, drip!—under that elm tree,
Though then it was young. Now it is old
But good, not like the barn and me.

To-morrow they cut it down. They will leave
The barn, as I shall be left, maybe.
What holds it up? 'Twould not pay to pull down.
Well, this place has no other antiquity.

No abbey or castle looks so old
As this that Job Knight built in '54,
Built to keep corn for rats and men.
Now there's fowls in the roof, pigs on the floor.

What thatch survives is dung for the grass,
The best grass on the farm. A pity the roof
Will not bear a mower to mow it. But
Only fowls have foothold enough.

Starlings used to sit there with bubbling throats
Making a spiky beard as they chattered
And whistled and kissed, with heads in air,
Till they thought of something else that mattered.

But now they cannot find a place,
Among all those holes, for a nest any more.
It's the turn of lesser things, I suppose.
Once I fancied 'twas starlings they built it for.

Collected Poems

Glamorgan

The man who knows Glamorgan knows Wales. It is a land of mountains much divided by rivers and rivulets, increasing in height and wildness inland, but having between the mountains and the sea a fertile border which varies from a few hundred yards to several miles in breadth. This fertile land is decorated by the large number of castles which once protected the Normans against the mountain Welshmen. The rivers supply large and numerous steel works, copper works, tinplate works, etc., and receive from them poison of many colours. The mountains are pierced by coal-mines and carved by quarries. Glamorgan possesses the great manufacturing towns and seaports of Cardiff and Swansea, the cathedral of Llandaff, the ancient townlet of Lantwit, and countless ruins, such as Neath Abbey, and the castles of Caerphilly, Coity, Kenfig, and Oystermouth. Some of its valleys, like those of Rhondda and Maesteg, are of the blackest; others, like that of Neath, are among the greenest; those of the Twrch and Mellte are very wild. It includes Llanmaes, one of the quietest places under the sun, as well as Dowlais and Tonypandy; and the large peninsula of Gower is shared between visitors and agriculture, though at the very edge of it stands Landore, where men have toiled for centuries to show what a town is when it is nothing but a town, where earth and air and river are chiefly dirt. It has yellow rivers like the Tawe, and rivers like the Perddin, the Camffrd and the Thaw, which are as living crystal where they are not white as milk. The coast is one of precipices, as throughout half of Gower; of sandhills, as at Porthcawl. It is a land of mines, of furnaces, and slums, but also of the richest and gentlest fields, as in the Vale of Glamorgan, still gleaming with the white houses which were praised hundreds of years ago by poets. And, east and west, there is hardly a hill-top but commands the sea.

Other counties have a similar variety of characters, but Glamorgan
shows them altogether in a hundred places. From the windmill tower
above Swansea, for example, you see the ships and the chimneys of
Swansea, Neath, and Port Talbot; but you see also, on the one hand,
corn, pasture, moorland, and white cottages, the rivers Neath and
Tawe cleaving with their romantic valleys a great realm of mountains;
on the other hand, the blue waters and yellow sands of a sea that ex-
tends thirty miles away southward to Exmoor. The same, or as much,
can be commanded from the neighbourhood of Cardiff, Pontypridd,
Neath, or Pontardulais. A composite portrait of the county would
show green fields, black fields, a hundred chimneys pouring out fire
and smoke, a white farm-house with its sheds and lodges shining like a
negro's teeth, and a background of mountains with cataracts among
their crags and fern. But composite portraits are without life. To com-
bine, for example, the Vale of Glamorgan with Morriston, Landore,
and Swansea is like mixing an apple with a lump of coal, which would
make neither food nor fuel. And yet you have often equally great con-
trasts side by side, especially during the first stages in the growth of a
place like Pontardulais*—when it is being transformed from a village
with a fulling-mill and an inn to a Hell, fully equipped. Then the
purest green fields border on the factory yard, and will be ready to en-
croach on it if deserted. The old white cottage of Glamorgan will stand
side by side with the cheapest town type, in which the mortar is made
with sand instead of coal. Where there used to be a live otter is now a
dead dog or two. By the little solitary farm under the four sycamores
the miner greets the shepherd, and the mountain sheep and their
lambs, which are prettier than deer, feed close to the smoke, provided
that the west wind carries it off the pasture, not on to it. These things
are to be found every year by anyone who walks twenty or thirty miles
in Glamorgan.

In the course of such a walk you see every variety. In the morning
you are in a green castle court which Owen Glendower visited; a horse
grazes among the tall fragments of masonry, draped with ivy, felted
with grass and daisy, tufted with little ash trees, and the blue of two
peacocks nodding across burns in the sunshine. A robin sings, the
rooks caw on their way to the stubble, the jackdaws chaff one another
in the clear sky above their woods. In the south lies the sea, in the north
the mountains; and the earth is as tranquil as the sky. You pass nothing

* Where E. T. often visited relatives.

worse all the morning than a quarry and golf-links. At midday you
have on your left the sand-dunes, on your right the mountains, to
which the trees, yellow and red and bare, are fitted like a bird's breast-
feathers. The curlews cry over the road as you approach factories and
ships, and a town of mean streets and enormous 'pubs', of bustle,
prosperity, and pale faces. Before evening you are in a valley of chimneys, skirting a wide, barren marsh, where black streamlets run, and
women search for something on the slopes of fuming slag-mountains.
Gradually, the turns of the valley reveal, first, a hundred tall stacks and
their attendant fleeces of smoke, white, black, or tawny, and then a
hundred masts and funnels, a crescent of yellow sand, the blue water
of Swansea Bay, with the Mumbles lighthouse to the right, and to the
left the horizontal white band of cottages on the red mountain above
Port Talbot, three miles away. In many other directions a similar walk
may be taken. The mountainous pit alone in which Swansea lies will
furnish, on a lesser scale, the same contrasting and yet combining
elements of grace, majesty, and horror, of blue sea and green hill, of
coal-mine, copper works, and slums. The town and its coast and hills
make as accurately as possible a composite portrait of Glamorgan. But
then it is also possible to spend a whole day within the county and
never quit the fern, heather, and whinberry of the stony mountains;
and another day in exuberant undulating country as sweet as Kent, but
bounded by mountains; and yet another without any variety except in
the smoke you breathe, the ashes you tread, the colour of the streams
and the number of the pit-mouths or chimneys in sight. To see it all is
to see Wales—I do not say to know it.

The Last Sheaf

Tall Nettles

Tall nettles cover up, as they have done
These many springs, the rusty harrow, the plough
Long worn out, and the roller made of stone:
Only the elm butt tops the nettles now.

This corner of the farmyard I like most:
As well as any bloom upon a flower
I like the dust on the nettles, never lost
Except to prove the sweetness of a shower.

Collected Poems

A Farmhouse

Having passed the ruined abbey and the orchard, I came to a long, low farmhouse kitchen, smelling of bacon and herbs and burning sycamore and ash. A gun, a blunderbuss, a pair of silver spurs, and a golden spray of last year's corn hung over the high mantelpiece and its many brass candlesticks; and beneath was an open fireplace and a perpetual red fire, and two teapots warming, for they had tea for breakfast, tea for dinner, tea for tea, tea for supper, and tea between. The floor was of sanded slate flags, and on them a long many-legged table, an oak settle, a table piano, and some Chippendale chairs. There were also two tall clocks; and they were the most human clocks I ever met, for they ticked with effort and uneasiness: they seemed to think and sorrow over time, as if they caused it, and did not go on thoughtlessly or impudently like most clocks, which are insufferable; they found the hours troublesome and did not twitter mechanically over them; and at midnight the twelve strokes always nearly ruined them, so great was the effort. On the wall were a large portrait of Spurgeon, several sets of verses printed and framed in memory of dead members of the family, an allegorical tree watered by the devil, and photographs of a bard and of Mr. Lloyd George. There were about fifty well-used books near the fire, and two or three men smoking, and one man reading some serious book aloud, by the only lamp; and a white girl was carrying out the week's baking, of large loaves, flat fruit tarts of blackberry, apple, and whinberry, plain golden cakes, large soft currant biscuits, and curled oat cakes. And outside, the noises of a west wind and a flooded stream, the whimper of an otter, and the long, slow laugh of an owl; and always silent, but never forgotten, the restless, towering outline of a mountain.

The fire was—is—of wood, dry oak-twigs of last spring, stout ash sticks cut this morning, and brawny oak butts grubbed from the copse years after the tree was felled. And I remember how we built it up one autumn, when the heat and business of the day had almost let it die.

We had been out all day, cutting and binding the late corn. At one moment we admired the wheat straightening in the sun after drooping in rain, with grey heads all bent one way over the luminous amber stalks, and at last leaning and quivering like runners about to start or like a wind made visible. At another moment we admired the gracious groups of sheaves in pyramids made by our own hands, as we sat and drank our buttermilk or ale, and ate bread and cheese or chwippod (the harvesters' stiff pudding of raisins, rice, bread, and fresh milk) among the furze mixed with bramble and fern at the edge of the field. Behind us was a place given over to blue scabious flowers, haunted much by blue butterflies of the same hue; to cross-leaved heath and its clusters of close, pensile ovals, of a perfect white that blushed towards the sun; to a dainty embroidery of tormentil shining with unvaried gold; and to tall, purple loosestrife, with bees at it, dispensing a thin perfume of the kind that all fair living things, plants or children, breathe.

What a thing it is to reap the wheat with your own hands, to thresh it with the oaken flail in the misty barn, to ride with it to the mill and take your last trout while it is ground, and then to eat it with no decoration of butter, straight from the oven! There is nothing better, unless it be to eat your trout with the virgin appetite which you have won in catching it. But in the field, we should have been pleased with the plainest meal a hungry man can have, which is, I suppose, barley bread and a pale 'double Caermarthen' cheese, which you cut with a hatchet after casting it on the floor and making it bounce, to be sure that it is a double Caermarthen. And yet I do not know. For even a Welsh hymnist of the eighteenth century, in translating 'the increase of the fields', wrote avidly of 'wheaten bread', so serious was his distaste for barley bread. But it was to a meal of wheaten bread and oat cake, and cheese and onions and cucumber, that we came in, while the trembling splendours of the first stars shone, as if they also were dewy like the furze. Nothing is to be compared with the pleasure of seeing the stars thus in the east, when most eyes are watching the west, except perhaps to read a fresh modern poet, straight from the press, before any one has praised it, and to know that it is good.

As we sat, some were singing the song 'Morwynion Sir Gaer-fyrddin'. Some were looking out at the old hay waggon before the gate.

Fine grass was already growing in corners of the wrecked hay waggon. Two months before, it travelled many times a day between the rick and the fields. Swallow was in the shafts while it carried all the village children to the field, as it had done some sixty years ago, when the village wheelwright helped God to make it. The waggoner lifted them out in clusters; the haymakers loaded silently; the waggon moved along the roads between the swathes; and, followed by children who expected another ride, and drawn by Swallow and Darling, it reached the rick that began to rise, like an early church, beside the elms. But hardly had it set out for another load than Swallow shied; an axle splintered and tore and broke in two, near the hub of one wheel, which subsided so that a corner of the waggon fell askew into the tussocks, and the suspended horse-shoe dropped from its place. There the mare left it, and switched her black tail from side to side of her lucent, nut-brown haunches, as she went.

All day the waggon was now the children's own. They climbed and slid and made believe that they were sailors, on its thin, polished timbers. The grass had grown up to it, under its protection. Before it fell, the massive wheels and delicate curved sides had been so fair and strong that no one thought of its end. Now, the exposed decay raised a smile at its so recent death. No one gave it a thought, except, perhaps, as now, when the September evening began, and one saw it on this side of the serious, dark elms, when the flooded ruts were gleaming, and a cold light fell over it from a tempestuous sky, and the motionless air was full of the shining of moist quinces and yellow fallen apples in long herbage; and, far off, the cowman let a gate shut noisily; the late swallows and early bats mingled in flight; and, under an oak, a tramp was kindling his fire. . . .

Suddenly in came the dog, one of those thievish, lean, swift, demi-wolves, that appear so fearful of meeting a stranger, but when he has passed, turn and follow him. He shook himself, stepped into the hearth and out and in again. With him was one whose red face and shining eyes and crisped hair were the decoration with which the wind invests his true lovers. A north wind had risen and given the word, and he repeated it: let us have a fire.

So one brought hay and twigs, another branches and knotted logs, and another the bellows. We made an edifice worthy of fire and kneeled with the dog to watch light changing into heat, as the spirals of sparks arose. The pyre was not more beautiful which turned to roses round the innocent maiden for whom it was lit; nor that more wonderful round which, night after night in the west, the clouds are solemnly ranged, waiting for the command that will tell them whither they are bound in the dark blue night. We became as the logs, that now and then settled down (as if they wished to be comfortable) and sent out, as we did words, some bristling sparks of satisfaction. And hardly did we envy then the man who lit the first fire and saw his own stupendous shadow in cave or wood and called it a god. As we kneeled, and our sight grew pleasantly dim, were we looking at fireborn recollections of our own childhood, wondering that such a childhood and youth as ours could ever have been; or at a golden age that never was? . . .

Wales

FIGURES IN
THE LANDSCAPE

A Wiltshire Molecatcher

In fresh clear air of the white dawn the grey mass of the distant hills rises out of the plain like a headland from the sea, and its outline is pencilled against the checkered sky, where fleecy clouds, red-tipped and flushed with pink, roll their fantastic shapes along the ridge. Black firs in a shattered group look blacker still in the brilliant white light. Peewits that were up ere the night gloom was broken by the first rays creeping over the hill, flap with an easy grace of wing from our path, and with a whirl of gay pinions begin an aerial dance, delighting in their unsurpassed nimbleness of flight. One tiny form, looming faintly as yet in the distance, darkens the grey slope. The molecatcher, nearing the end of his early round, descends to the valley now where his remotest traps are set. A grey-complexioned, silent man he is, with a curious lingering gait, ever looking downward as he goes. On these wide open hills there is hardly a man without woodcraft enough to know the ways of his fellow-denizens of the waste, and, if need be, the way to set up a wire. The molecatcher is no exception, and long use compels him to watch the sward at his feet. Dark grizzled curls hang about his low, deeply-furrowed brow, while his neck, freckled and hard, is open to the wind. His back is bent rather from constant stooping than from age, and there is power in him yet, as you may note when he climbs the hill.

Of all the molecatcher's odd attire—thirdhand velveteen jacket, torn loose gaiters, and stained corduroys—his hat is the most curious. Made of soft felt, it was once white, but is now weathered to lichen-grey, and with darker streaks winding here and there; the broad brim curves downward and overhangs his forehead, shadowing all his face. Save when he looks up, half of his shaggy visage is hidden, and this concealment adds to the mystery that clings to a man of his decaying profession. By the bent brim of his hat, his curls of growing years, and by his dense eyebrows, his eyes are half hidden, as are the mole's by its protecting fur. Unperceived, the keen small eyes are ever fixed upon you; and the stranger shrinks on becoming conscious of their piercing glance through the shadow hanging about his face. Rarely, even in conversation, is the veil of mystery removed. It may be that he carries secrets which shall die with him; so, at least, his morose reserve suggests. Not without a natural dignity, in spite of his lowly occupation, he goes through his day of silent solitary toil, or holds short pithy snatches of talk with those who care to visit him. Seated in the mound, between high double hedges, at noon over his 'dinner', luxuriously pillowed among lush grass and golden pilewort, with his back leaning against an elm, he will converse intelligently on subjects that might have been deemed beyond his care, with a sharpness of sense and economy of words that bespeak a healthy mind cleansed by the pure hillside air.

Far up on the plain that undulates beyond this ridge of Wiltshire downland, acres of pasture are brown with the mole's crowded earthworks. Amid this desolation not even the thistle flourishes, and the crows, playing bo-peep among the heaps, must find only scanty fare. But it is in the lowland meadows, rather than on the bleak bare hills, that the molecatcher finds his hunting-ground. There he can sit, when the early thaw winds set the moles at work by loosening the iron grip of the frost, and can watch the trap spring as the creature is silently crushed or garotted. On the hill, even when the mild winds are blowing, it is cold work enough, and rarely do the traps spring soon after they are set. Generally the moles are busiest at night, and it is then that the wholesale captures are made which threaten to exterminate the velvety burrower. Constant passing through the earth seems rather to sleek the fur than to coarsen it, but in almost every case the mole is infested with minute insects which disappear when the body is removed from the trap. The old-fashioned noose, tightened by the springing of a lissom wand stuck in the ground, has been generally superseded by an iron trap, having two pairs of jaws which close, one or the other, round the creature's body as he attempts to force a way through a hole not large enough to admit him.

The level green of the meadow is ruffled with the brown of many mole-heaps, scattered like miniature mountain chains and groups here and there in disarray. Of these some are old, as may be guessed from their smoothness, and the newly-springing growth of buttercup or grass which has risen through the mould. Those that are new show the colour of the fresh-turned soil, and are bare of vegetation. But beside the little mounds—'wont 'yeps' or 'oont heaves', the molecatcher calls them—the moles, like all wild creatures, have their regular runs, by which their journeyings can be traced. Frequently these runs are close beneath the surface, and the earth is turned up throughout their length, so that, by removing the broken sods, the tunnel may be revealed, rounded, and large enough to admit the hand for some distance. At times, indeed, they may be tracked for a short space over the grass without any disturbance of the soil. As the runs always range from heap to heap—the latter being the result of the pushing out of the borings—even where they do not cut up the ground, they can be discovered by probing with a stick, unless unusually deep. The mole-catcher makes a deep heel-mark on the run—pressing the earth together, and so blocking the tunnel—and is thus able to tell when the mole has passed that way by the consequent lifting of the trodden turf. Two moles never, it is said, meet snout to snout underground without a fight, which invariably ends in the death of one combatant. In one of these heaps, usually somewhat larger than the rest, the mole brings forth its young, whose fate is often to be pitched rudely out on to the sward as they lie in their dark nests. Runs are often to be seen which mark the turf in a long line, seldom interrupted by heaps, and in such the molecatcher prefers to set his traps. A dozen moles is no very rare number to be caught without long interval in a single tunnel, and it has been known to reach as many as seventeen.

The long track is more likely to be used than the short one, and is the mole's highway, or main road, from which he seldom turns aside, except to make fresh burrowings. Meadows are often intersected in places by twisting runs, and it is hard for the trapper to decide which to use. He may have to wait several days ere the animal passes that way. In search of insect food, moles will wander to the strangest places, boring hard-trodden paths, and even stony roads. Occasionally, in all likelihood, they pass under brooks and watercourses; and gardens parted from the fields by roads and walls are commonly disturbed by their heaps. In the garden mole-runs mingle with the tunnelling of the smaller field-mice, who mine for beans and other garden seeds. Far plainer than rabbit-paths, by reason of the turned-up mould, which makes them patent to all, mole-runs sometimes extend for several score yards, either straight or with devious curves, just as the chance of food or soil influences the burrower. As the year advances, and, with summer heats and drought, the soil becomes hard and dry, the number of surface-runs decreases, and the molecatcher must put aside his traps, or be content with a few chance captures. The ground at the top is then more difficult to work: worms also, and the insects which are the mole's staple food, descend with the moisture into the earth, and the mole must follow them or starve.

The molecatcher's grey-clad figure stands out on the hill-slope, brilliant with the morning sun, like a dead and wrinkled thorn, seeming scarcely to move. He crosses a clover-field, where the scanty growth does not quite hide the chalk, and on a nearer approach the hares' runs show faintly as light streaks across the mingled green and grey and white. Days go by without a single visitor to the remoter parts of these broad hills, and the molecatcher may safely stoop in his path to take the hare which has lain in the wire since daybreak. The weathered coat flaps in the wind as the hare sinks into the unsuspected pocket concealed by the ample velveteen, and, quietly as ever, the climb continues. Though he stoops, and his gaze seems always directed downward, he will note, as he looks intuitively up, the swift plovers that whistle and rush with their wings as they seek the ploughlands of the valley. Like a dim cloud, alone on the ridge, the old man sinks out of sight beyond where the smooth mounds of the ancient 'castle' swell into the blue.

The Woodland Life

A Widow

In the cottage lived a mother and son. She was very little and very old. Her hair was still dark brown, her eyes almost as dark, her skin not quite so dark as her eyes, a nut-brown woman, lean, sweet, and wholesome-looking as a nut. She might often be seen sitting and looking to the south-west when a gap in the hills framed a vision of mountain peaks twenty miles beyond; and always she smiled a little. A passer-by might have thought that she never did anything but sit inside or outside the open door unless he had noticed the whiteness of the stones and the polish on the metal in the room where she had for fifty years collected things that could be polished. Few ever saw Catherine Anne at work save her son, and he not often, for he was away early and home late. He left her entirely alone, visited of none unless on days when the smart tradesman strode up the path, deposited her weekly packages on the table while he commented on the weather, and then replacing his pencil behind his ear bade her 'Good Afternoon' in English. It was one of the few English remarks to which she could reply in English. Her only other English words were 'beautiful' and 'excursion train'. For though some of the brown in her face was a gift of tropics sun in the days when she sailed with her husband on his ship, she had learned nothing but Welsh. The old man, so she called him though dead these forty years, had been against her learning English. A God-knowing and God-fearing Methodist, he had seen in that tongue the avenue through which his beautiful young wife might receive the knowledge of good and evil. After his death at sea she had of her own accord refused all contact with the thing, and now when it was all around her she never moved from the house. Her son knew it, but at home he spoke the native idiom, and when she heard him she seemed to be once more in her father's house, or in the orchard where little red apples overhung the rocky brook at the mountain foot. There it was that she gained, no one knows how, the nourishment from mother earth that gave her the deep contentment expressed in her health and her smile, in the shining metal, and in her patience—which was not endurance or torpor—patience of an order that seemed to be all but extinct in the world. Memory and hope were at balance in the brain that looked out of her brown eyes, and the present moment, often dull-seeming or even unkind, did not exist for her. Those eyes never closed while she sat by her door, and it might be conjectured that as she gazed east and north and west she saw more than the white stones and yellow stonecrop, the alders and royal fern, the hedge following the road, the lean oak trees among the rocks, the farther hills and their curlews and cairns, the sky, and now and then the uttermost mountains, which were all that an observer could see. If the casual observer waited more than a few moments in summer he might see that she was never quite alone. The air between her and the hills was the playground of several pairs of black swifts, wheeling and leaping round and up and down and straight forward, so that the bluest sky was never blank or the brightest grass without a shadow. Out of these birds two often screamed down precipitously to the white cottage and disappeared in their nests under the thatch above her head. Catherine Anne smiled a little more at these sudden stormy visits, and there were times when it seemed certain that she received others, though neither visible nor audible.

Some thought that she believed the swifts to be some kind of spirits,

and one who was very wise said that if Catherine Anne Jones had been
cleverer she might have been a wicked woman.

Rest and Unrest

The Huxter

He has a hump like an ape on his back;
He has of money a plentiful lack;
And but for a gay coat of double his girth
There is not a plainer thing on the earth
    This fine May morning.

But the huxter has a bottle of beer;
He drives a cart and his wife sits near
Who does not heed his lack or his hump;
And they laugh as down the lane they bump
    This fine May morning.

Collected Poems

The Poacher

I wish to make a nice distinction between poachers and poachers. The
man who is nothing but a poacher I regard as one only in the strict
literal sense. Such a man is rare today. Formerly he went to the woods
as another man went to the Bar. He lived like a gentleman upon other
men's venison, and was beneath the pleasure of salt-pork broth. He
would swagger about the hamlet with a deer on his back. The deer was
but a carcass at sixpence the pound to him. He has lately stooped to
dictate his autobiography, which may be bought over the counter. A
less majestical note was never sounded. He turned gamekeeper, and no
doubt touched his cap for half-a-sovereign, and stared at his palm for a
crown. He is, in short, 'one of God's creatures'. But the nobler one I
have in mind seemed to bear high office in the scheme of the natural
world. A mighty man, capable of killing anything and of sparing anything too, he was a true scholar in his kind. The pedants who peep and

botanize and cry 'allium' or 'enicus' to one another in the awful woods, and the sublime enthusiasts who cannot see the earth for the flowers, were equally beneath him. He would give twelve hours a day at least to the open air, as a scholar to his books. Thus he had acquired a large erudition which would probably have exhausted a whole field of in-quiry if written down. It is fortunate that faultless observers like this hand down nothing to posterity, since it leaves us in these latter days free to feel ourselves discoverers when we come upon what hundreds have known during the last thousand years. In the case of this man, the knowledge came out not so much in speech—of which he was economical—as in infinite tact,

> *Wearing all that weight*
> *Of learning lightly like a flower.*

It was shown in the way he stepped in the woods, in the way he laid his ear to the bare ground (not the grass) to ascertain a distant noise of footsteps. I have seen him lose a wood-pigeon by an interrupted aim, and, standing without sound or motion, shoot the bird, that returned to its branch, enchanted by the absence of hostile sounds; for his very clothes were more the work of nature than the tailor, and matched the trees like a hawk or a November moth. His belief in the earth as a living thing was almost a superstition. I shall not forget how he took me to a hilltop one autumn day, when the quiet gave birth to sound after sound as we listened and let our silence grow. By a process of elimination he set aside the wind, the birds, the falling leaves, the water, and tried to capture for my sake the low hum which was the earth making music to itself. And what I heard I can no more describe than the magic of an excellent voice when once it is silent. 'Depend upon it, that means something,' he said. 'And now—' there was a sharp report and a hare that I had not noticed bounded as if it had fallen from a great height, and lay dead.

Having been caught once, I remarked that his captor must have been a clever man. 'A fool,' he replied—'a fool. He'd been after me a hundred times, and I had fooled him all but once.' It was at one time his practice to deliver a tithe of his poached game at the cottages of the sick, infirm, or poor, *as a present from the Squire*, a notoriously un-generous man. His occupation had made him indifferent to the future or the past. None ever chattered less about past happiness and future pain. He seemed to owe a duty to the present moment of which he

D

partook as if he were eating ripe fruit. Even a piece of drudgery or a keen sorrow never drove his intelligence backward or forward; pain he took as some take medicine, on trust. Thus he was a small, though not a poor, talker. Venturing once to greet him pleasantly with the long beginning of a story, when I found him seated without any visible occupation, and noticing his irritation, I said that I had supposed he was not doing anything; to which he answered 'Yes, nothing!' and continued. At one time of his life he heard that a considerable sum of money had been left to him. A year later, the foundering of a ship left his fortunes unchanged; and on the afternoon of the news, he shot every pigeon at which he raised his gun. Birds of prey he would never shoot, even to show his skill. Jackdaws were always spared; he used to say that there was 'a bit of God' in that bird. It was noticeable, too, that here and there he spared game birds, though he despised the race. I have seen him raise his gun and drop it again, not without a sigh as the bird flew off, observing that there was 'something in the bird' which stayed his hand. In men, as in birds and beasts, he was anxious to see individuality, and loved the creature that possessed and used it. The only time I ever saw him use contempt was towards a beggar who had soiled his calling by theft. A good beggar, a good thief, anything beyond which 'the force of nature could no further go,' he reverenced. And he was a good poacher, glorying in the name. He died polishing the white steel on his gun.

Wales

A Gentle Craftsman

My friend had twice hooked me; the parson had risen to a March brown, and in fact been hooked; but I failed to land, thus losing the only chance of an overflowing creel. For some hours we had been sowing the wind with flies. The busy nut-brown water of the ripples barely wetted the stones, and could not hold a trout. The pools, that had been glass all day, were changed to silver by the great splendour of twilight; over them now and then wavered a flash as of swords unsheathed for a moment, where the large trout leapt. (Yet the biggest fish of the season had just been landed below us by a clothes-line and a rod like 'the mast of some great amiral'.) The rise and fall of the greenheart, the tossing of the silk as it evolves a perfectly straight line out of subtlest curves, always exert a kind of sorcery, to which your own silence ministers, amid all the jewel and blossom of summer in the grass and air. At twilight the sorcery is reinforced. The mere excellence of casting achieved by that time of day encourages you to go on. And when you stop—perhaps to change a fly—you are too deep in the enchantment to resist.

It had been a day that made us all more than happy, as if it were the beginning of 'the world's great age'. It was well to be there, as we were—

If the dream lasts 'twill turn the age to gold

The twilight was peculiarly fine. A casual passer-by would have detected the hum of gnats, the liquid whisper of poplars, the far-off sea speaking in muffled under-breath, or the snipping sound of bats. We, ourselves, had noticed them at first, and yet, without ceasing, they had mingled and combined into the orchestral silence of summer. Along with the night a mist was coming, and through it the moon and stars were white. We were casting all the time mechanically, dreamily. Overhead we could hear the lost, mournful voices of plovers that wandered invisible. Insects grew horribly bold, and stayed to be crushed by the hand that was meant to drive them off. The bats came closer and closer—some of them followed our flies in the air—one, indeed, hooked itself and fell. For a short time there was something diabolic in the air, in the shapes around us, and in the fancies that came. Was there not an elvish leer traced on the silver bark of the birch we passed just now? I confess that when a thought of the outer world did come, it was heartily to wish ourselves at the Three Dragons. There was a sense of stealthy preparation in the silence. There might be ghosts abroad, or something solemn was happening near at hand. Or were we come suddenly on fairy-land?

This is the fairy land—
We talk with goblins, owls, and elvish sprites,

As if we had passed into a strange land. We really seemed to be suspected by the things around, for the cattle stepped gradually up to our side, sniffed us, and would not be repulsed. I could scent the fume of a pernicious and alluring herb. Now and then, as before, a fish rose.

We longed for the splash to linger, so haunting was the silence become.

A home-returning miner came to our release, and we were glad of his company for a mile. He, too, had observed 'something funny' in the air just there. "Tis the ale at the Three Dragons, I'm thinking', was his conclusion, as he left.

As a fitting anodyne to our experiences, we determined to call on Captain Rowland, a worshipful old man, and master of the gentle craft, who lived near in a great house in a wood, where he cheated *ennui* with some choice books and a cabinet of tea cups,

With antic shapes in China's azure dy'd

The house, indeed, we found, but the Captain was gone. We had forgotten that it was five years since our last meeting. The walls of the garden were levelled and overgrown with moss, the famous 'little red apples' were still unpicked. Ivy had dislocated the masonry, and towered above the chimney in a gloomy pavilion of umbrage and flower. The house itself was a possession of nettles. Nothing remained save the superb ancestral turf, whose inconspicuous beauty—like the Captain's antique courtesy—had grown up in the family seat, as the result of peaceful centuries that scarcely raised an echo in the world.

In the village I learned that he was dead. It was hard to learn more, for he was generally loved, and his gamekeeper who knew him best, could not speak of him without distress.

He lived a bachelor in the great old house until he died. At home, he was a sharp-tempered, indolent, yet always occupied man, with rosy carbuncled face, who swore freely. It was easier for him to forget than to forgive. 'Who could love one that never made an enemy?' was a favourite question of his, to which an answer was not expected. I have noticed also that those who suffered oftenest by his temper loved him best. Yet he was not, in the ordinary sense, a generous man; his charity began and ended at home.

For days together he would sit in one room, smoking over theology, night-capped, slippered, wearing a waistcoat whose folds were a diary of years past in vigorous characters. Into this faded room he used to summon his household before the dinner-hour, when he read aloud to them—an odd solemnity—a passage from the *Newgate Calendar* in a stormy bass voice. At the more terrible parts the maids were asked to conceal their faces. 'Amen,' he bellowed, at the end. 'Amen,' whispered the trembling assembly. 'And now, if you like, you can go to church,' was his valediction on Sundays.

He was seldom abroad, save to fish, and out of doors he was metamorphosed. He then invariably wore black clothes, a tall silk hat, and a white cravat. His attitude was in accord. He would sit, amid the Hosannahs of jubilant Nature, as summer passed into the land, like an old tree beside the stream, like a figure in a frieze—

With marble men and maidens overwrought.

Whilst fishing he never spoke a word, nor would he accept society, though the most sociable of men. 'Fishing is fishing,' he used to say, elliptically. Youthful and feminine anglers he gravely hated; the latter, I think, because they sometimes laughed aloud in their triumphs. According to the Captain, whatever the *casus belli*, war was declared against fish. The rules of warfare must be obeyed. You must play the game as if (or, the Captain said, 'because') your opponents were intellectual and moral creatures. A fish accidentally hooked he returned to the water; and yet, I admit, it was his glory to pull the same out again by fair play. It was significantly whispered in the neighbourhood that unless Captain Rowland was out no fish would be caught.

His only fault was his scorn of the *Compleat Angler*. 'The old liar,' he exclaimed: 'but,' he said, softening, 'a setter of nightlines is beneath contempt.' Secretly, I believe, he loved the book. Only he would not countenance the man who was first a lover of the picturesque, and merely, in the second place, an angler. 'There are too many of them,' was his opinion; 'besides, they pick my daffodils and ruin the fruit trees when they ask leave to sit in the orchard and hear the nightingale.'

I loved the man for certain invaluable delusions, which formed his philosophy, and, being one of the poor objects of his scorn, I am grateful to him for taking me to many a delicate place on the whistling moors —under the woods, in 'the morning world's fresh gold', or when the noonday heat defrauds the lilies of their dew—and in the meadows beside the still waters.

Rose Acre Papers

A Swindon Family
⊸⊱

Swindon was a thousand times better. It was delicious to pass Wantage, Challow, Uffington, Shrivenham, to see the 75th, 76th mile marks by the railwayside, to slow down at last to the cry of 'Swindon' and see my grandmother, my uncle or my aunt waiting. My aunt was an attendant in the refreshment bar, and sometimes gave me a cake or sandwich to eat amid the smell of spirits, or took me to the private apartments, talking in a high bright voice and showing me round to various other neat women in black with high bright voices and nothing but smiles and laughs. My uncle was a fitter in the Great Western Railway works and knew everybody. He was tall, easy-going, and had a pipe in his mouth and very likely a dog at his heels. I was proud to be with him as he nodded to the one-legged signalman and the man with a white apron and a long hammer for tapping the wheels of all the carriages.

The look of the town pleased me altogether. I could think no ill of houses built entirely of stone instead of brick, especially as they seemed to exist chiefly to serve as avenues by which I happily approached to my grandmother's. It was for me a blessed place. The stonework, the flowers in the gardens, the Wiltshire accent, the rain if it was raining, the sun if it was shining, the absence of school and schoolmaster and of most ordinary forms of compulsion—everything was paradisal. No room ever was as cosy as my grandmother's kitchen. Its open range was always bright. There was a pair of bellows frequently in use. A brass turnspit hung from under the mantelpiece. The radiant steel trivet was excellent in itself but often bore a load of girdle cakes or buttered toast or more substantial things. An old brown earthenware teapot stood eternally upon the hob. Tea-caddies, brass candlesticks, clay pipes and vases full of spills, stood on the mantelpiece. On its walls hung coloured engravings entitled 'Spring' and 'Summer' and painted in England some time before the Fall, and photographs of me and Mr. Gladstone's Cabinets and Mr. Gladstone, of Belle Bitton, and of an uncle who had died long before I was born. There were chairs and there was an old mahogany table piano at one side. The smell of

'Westward Ho' tobacco hung about the room. My uncle got us chatting instantly. He seemed grown up, yet a boy, by the way he laughed, whistled and sang a bit of a gay tune. At supper, with our bread and cheese, or cold bacon, or hot faggots, or chitterlings, and pickles, he would now and then give us a little tumbler, or 'tot', of ale.

My grandmother being all important, omnipotent, omnipresent if not omniscient, she stood out less. She marketed, cooked, cleaned, did everything. She made pies with pastry a full inch thick, and many different undulant fruit tarts on plates. Above all, she made doughy cakes, of dough, allspice and many raisins, which were as much better than other cakes as Swindon was better than other towns, and always as much better than other so-called doughy cakes. She knew, too, where to get butter which taught me how divine a thing butter can be made. On the other hand, she was a Conservative and a churchwoman. Without her, these holidays would have been impossible, and she gave me countless pleasures. But if I loved her it was largely because of these things, not instinctively or because she loved me. She was marvellously kind and necessary but we were never close together; and, when there was any quarrel, contempt mingled with my hate of her inheritance from semi-rural Wales of George the Fourth's time. She was bigoted, worldly, crafty, narrow-minded, and ungenerous, as I very early began to feel. She read her Bible and sang hymns to herself, sometimes in Welsh. She also sang Welsh songs that were not hymns, in particular one that an old beggar used to sing at Tredegar when she was a girl, something about a son whom the mother was begging not to be married. When she wanted to warn me against going fishing some miles off with a strange man she hinted that he might be Jack the Ripper.

She first took me to church. Clad in those uncomfortable clothes, I walked beside her, who looked more uncomfortable in her layers of black. I felt that everyone enjoyed being stiff, solemn, black, except myself. On entering the church she bent forward to pray, dragging me down with her to blur my sight for a similar period. I rose with an added awkwardness in gazing at the grim emotionless multitudes of hats, bonnets, and bare heads. It was an inexplicable conspiracy for an hour's self-torture. The service was a dreary discomfort in which the hymns were green isles. When all was over, we crept with a shuffle, a pause, a shuffle, a pause, out to the tombstones and the astonishing fresh light. I was introduced to other women and discussed. I was always being told how like my mother I was and how tall for my age. My grandmother took me to several old Welshwomen, and they all said, 'He's a regular——.' They used to remark how well my father was doing, my grandfather who had long been dead having only been a fitter. To hide something from me, they spoke in Welsh. Sometimes I was more elaborately shown off. Behind a shop smelling of bacon, butter and acid sweets, I stood up before a stout woman smelling a little less strongly of the same, to recite 'The Charge of the Light Brigade'. My reward was a penny or a screw of sweets. The only visit of this kind which I enjoyed was to a farmhouse a mile away, though I can only recall the walk, the various gates, the best parlour with a Bible in the window between the lace curtains, and the glass of warm milk. Between her and my uncle who kept the house going I saw much bickering. Spending most of his evenings out at club or public-house, he neglected the garden and I dare say other things. I dimly knew that he was usually courting a farmer's daughter somewhere a few miles out, not always the same one. Sometimes when I was walking with him the girl appeared and joined us and at twilight I returned alone.

The little ivy-covered house, therefore, though I enjoyed the meals and evenings there, was above all a convenient centre for games and rambles. In my earlier visits the rambles of any length were on a Sunday with my uncle. He and I and usually my next brother who was two years younger would set out after a late breakfast. The Club was the first stop. It seemed to be full of grown men in a good temper and very much like schoolboys over their ale, their pipes of shag or 'Westward Ho', their *Reynolds News*. My uncle would tell them a little about us. They chaffed us. The men talked or whispered. Then before we were really impatient my uncle drained his glass and we got on to the canal-side and out of the town, not without greetings or a word or two from men lounging in their back-gardens over their vegetables, their fowls and pigeons. We kept to the canal for a mile or two, and sometimes another man joined us. The roach played in the deep green streams among the reeds, many of them bigger than any fish we had ever caught, here and there a monster. Better still my uncle would discover a long thin jack close inshore, as if anchored. If it did not shoot out with a kick and a swirl of water my uncle probably aimed at it with a stone. One great jack excited us by leaping again and again out of the water, at times so near the bank that we made sure he was ours. But the chief Sunday sport was with water rats. We were fascinated as men

yelled encouragements, threats, advice, or praises, and a terrier swam
down a rat in spite of its divings. When no dog was handy a rat surprised in mid-stream was a good mark for a stone, a snake's head a more
difficult one. The moorhens in the reeds had no more mercy from
them, but more often than not escaped. A dead dog was a good deal
better than nothing. Not that we were unhappy without something
for a mark. We threw flat stones to make ducks and drakes along the
sunny water, or sheltering from rain under one of the low stone bridges
plunged heavy stones with all our might down into the black depth.

Alongside the canal were many narrow copses of oak with underwood of ash and willow, the resorts of lovers and gamblers. The
pleasantest thing I ever did in them at that time was to peel rings off the
bark of a willow stick, in imitation of a carter's brass-ringed whip.
My uncle taught us. He could also fashion a whistle by slipping the
bark whole off a section of willow, but I never could. Or he made a
'cat' or 'catty' by tapering both ends of a round stick six inches long.
Hit at one end by a downward blow from a longer stick the cat rose
spinning up into the air and had then to be slashed horizontally as far
as possible. My uncle could play tipcat better than any boy. In these
copses or in the hedges or roadside trees, as we went along, he pointed
out the nests.

And then at one o'clock after another visit to the Club, home to a
dinner of lamb, green peas, and mint-sauce, followed by rhubarb and
custard.

Perhaps it was a little later that I first went out fishing with my uncle.
He had not the patience of a fisherman. But there was nothing he did
not know: the very winch that he used was made in the factory sur-
reptitiously. He caught roach, and before long I followed him. Even
better than this was the sport of seeing him confound the water bailiff
who asked for his licence. What with gay lies, chaff and threats, the
man had to go. We feared nothing at my uncle's side.

These, however, were special week-end delights, for Saturday afternoons or Sundays. The rest of the week was spent mainly in the streets,
on the canal-side adjacent, and in the nearer meadows. I liked seeing the
thousands of men going by on pavement and roadway for ten minutes
before work started and after it ended at the factory. The variety of
staid men and jaunty men, old men and boys, tall and stocky men, the
frowners and the smilers, fascinated me with endless indolent in-
articulate half-conjectures; and suddenly out of the multitude my uncle

—or for a moment once or twice a man extremely like him. Straight out of that mysterious pageant, the one positively and entirely living one, he used to come into the house, into the kitchen, into his chair and begin to eat.

The slower thinner weekly procession to market was the other great sight. Curious wizened old men with old hats, enormously stout women with shawls and black bonnets, smiling rosy ones with feathers, drove by. Their little carts were laden with eggs, butter, fowls, rabbits, and vegetables, from Lydiard and Shaw and Purton and Wootton Bassett. One or two always stopped at our gate, and the woman came to the door with a broad flat basket of eggs or butter under a cloth, and, very rarely, some mushrooms. She said, 'Good morning. How are you this morning? Got your little grandson here again. Nice weather we're having. Mustn't grumble. Yes, the butter's one-and-two now. . . .' While my grandmother went for her purse I stood at the open door and looked at the shrewd cheerful woman or at her dog who had come for a moment from under the cart. She with her cheerful and shrewd slow way was as strange and attractive as any poet's or romancer's woman became afterwards, as far away from my world. I never knew her name, nor did she use ours.

The Childhood of Edward Thomas

The Gypsy

A fortnight before Christmas Gypsies were everywhere:
Vans were drawn up on wastes, women trailed to the fair.
'My gentleman,' said one, 'you've got a lucky face.'
'And you've a luckier,' I thought, 'if such a grace
And impudence in rags are lucky.' 'Give a penny
For the poor baby's sake.' 'Indeed I have not any
Unless you can give change for a sovereign, my dear.'
'Then just half a pipeful of tobacco can you spare?'
I gave it. With that much victory she laughed content.
I should have given more, but off and away she went
With her baby and her pink sham flowers to rejoin
The rest before I could translate to its proper coin

Gratitude for her grace. And I paid nothing then,
As I pay nothing now with the dipping of my pen
For her brother's music when he drummed the tambourine
And stamped his feet, which made the workmen passing grin,
While his mouth-organ changed to a rascally Bacchanal dance
'Over the hills and far away.' This and his glance
Outlasted all the fair, farmer, and auctioneer,
Cheap-jack, balloon-man, drover with crooked stick, and steer,
Pig, turkey, goose, and duck, Christmas corpses to be.
Not even the kneeling ox had eyes like the Romany.
That night he peopled for me the hollow wooded land,
More dark and wild than stormiest heavens, that I searched and
    scanned
Like a ghost new-arrived. The gradations of the dark
Were like an underworld of death, but for the spark
In the Gypsy boy's black eyes as he played and stamped his tune,
'Over the hills and far away', and a crescent moon.

Collected Poems

A Man of the Woods

Long years of soldiering, tilling the soil, gamekeeping, and poaching
o' nights, moulded our man of the woods to what we find him now in
a hale, iron old age. In the education of such a man, not one of these
elements could have been spared; all will be found deeply essential.
Without the drill and exposure of a soldier's life, his back would never
have been so straight, nor his step so true, nor his eye so instantly
correct; and it again gave him an insight, also, into phases of life on
which he will begin to dwell, in a chattering senility, when sermons are
uttered more and more frequently from the grandfather's chair. Tilling
the soil was slow, certain preparation for the interchangeable crafts of
poacher and gamekeeper. It was then that, in the lengthened dinner-
hours under the summer sky, he could glean unutterable lore of the
hare and his many ways. Partridges nested in his master's fields, and it
needed no more than ordinary care to mark their lines of travel, their
hours of home-coming and outgoing, and their favoured corners

when the coveys packed in the time of the ripening hazel-nuts. At odd hours, in his tiny youth, opportunities were his to learn something of the economies of the smaller wild things of the hedgerows and leas; the thronging of strange racketing birds to the red October hips—these, the fieldfares, he called 'felts'—and the advent of the nightingale in earliest April to the spinney or the hazel-nook. He had been something of a favourite with the hunt; received valuable commissions which kept him in silent places, where the only stir was the 'rattle' which he whirled to turn the followed fox from a known retreat of his that could not be blocked. There, with occasions innumerable, answered by desires, he learned much, and reasoned, too, in his unguided way, and developed a tenderness towards wild creatures which was often in contrast with freaks of heedlessness. This tenderness stays with him now; he remembers the caged dormouse clicking for food over him, even in his nightly armchair. Keepering and poaching rank together in his education. Both gave him intricacies of knowledge in woodcraft that are impossible otherwise. Had he been a worse keeper, he would never have made so good a poacher; a worse poacher, and he were a useless keeper. Education, and 'better manners', he will say, have been the means of reducing the frequency of poaching, or, at least of the loud, bold poaching which he knew—desperate attacks of desperate men. Many such he recalls when the price of bread was high and wages low; cruel times for his class, he moans yet. Then a certain moodiness took hold of the cottagers; a dull, stubborn carelessness; and murderous affrays were the results. Such times have gone, he thinks, like the coast-war with smugglers. It is a memory of his that banded labourers in the cold winters of the years of the Crimea attacked the game woods. The raids called for unusual preparations against their success, and keepers sat or stood up in the covers all night in silence behind suspended sacks as protection from the wind. Nights like these ruined and bowed many good men.

Picture him in his woods; for he has been a man of the woods all his life, and is so yet. Wild, full locks whiten his brown neck and cheeks; a beard graces his chin. His eyes have the cold pale-blue brightness, suggestive of weak or short sight, which is almost always noticeable in men whose eyes are much used out of doors. The power of these eyes is genius, or instinct; their characteristic is that they realize everything in their sweep, noting details which ordinary vision would not appreciate or be conscious of. His gaze is inevitably and surely arrested by whatsoever moves within his ken; he knows that the rush-tufts dappling the hills are not the hares he seeks, but he also knows that they are rushtufts; nothing can escape him, and he makes certain, by an unconscious effort, of all he sees. Yet his glance is as rapid as possible; taking in, using or rejecting, what he sees, is the work of an inappreciable moment of time. He is little above the middle height, but his straight build gives him the appearance of being taller, and makes him what he is, a powerful man, whose strength is accompanied by agility, weight by speed. He has always been a runner; boasts, too, of his father's prowess across country. And one of the signs of his own enduring strength is that his breath is still good; he can run, if necessary, and mount the Downs, or climb a pollard-willow yet. He may tell you that 'the rheumatics' trouble him, but we find how much that means in a long tramp in the nutting season, up and down, over brooks and ha-has: then he is the last to complain, for the excitement of youth over the gipsying is as strong as ever in him. His dress, though he knows it not, by a curious but natural adaptation to surroundings, has become of unspeakable hues; slowly he has taken the colours of the wildwood in autumn's grey and brown, like the lizard in its native fern and parched rock or sward. Reminiscences of bird's-nesting raids are about him; undoubted evidences of his trespassing, in the stains of the keeper's 'tar trap'; sand, from the quarries, where an owl occupied two martins' tunnels whose partition slipped; lichen from the oaks, and green mould from the beeches where we sup. Many, many colours impress his sunburnt coat, his hat no less; unlike the Downs of his nativity, his cloth has emeralded in the sunshine.

He is a sportsman, with knowledge of a gun, but a better poacher, we confess; a fisherman, who can bait a hook, yet a better 'tickler' of tench and trout. In fishing he shows a failing that is often conspicuous in men used, as he is, to other methods and waters; he has too much slow patience—fonder, with rod in hand, of a joke than of his sport, and of the moorhen paddling than of either; he will sit for hours with no encouragement but 'something in the air' to keep him at his work. David is a naturalist, yet something of a quack—knows and loves the gold agrimony wand or the pilewort, February's star, but fears nightshade and brooklime more. On the subject of herbs, he is, of course, superstitiously old-fashioned, daring not to doubt; to him they are infallible. The same reverence for the sweet, small gifts of Nature makes him over-ready oftentimes to find 'Tongues in trees, books in the running brooks; Sermons in stones, and good in everything.' His 'tongues', there found, are too often dumb or vain; his 'books' might be deemed idle; but good he does find, and communicates with rare simplicity. His love of the greenwood is, in very fact, deep-seated. The superstition of our man of the woods with regard to herbs is allied to his speculation about birds; but it is only the speculation of almost all dwellers in the country. Just as the old people know there are tree magpies, and bush magpies, so he will have it that the 'twink' is other than the 'piefinch'; yet his twink, evidently named from the chaffinch's cry, makes a similar nest to the piefinch, and is as dainty in its use of lichen. 'Piefinch' is a common West Country name for the chaffinch. The songs, the call-notes, the flights, the habits, sociable or solitary, of wild birds are known to him. His imitations of the cries of wood-landers and birds of the field are exquisitely close; their consummation is in his rendering of the bullfinch's melancholy 'pipe', and of the young rook's clamour, swallowing a worm.

The old man's vocabulary is mixed and strange; many of its words being untraceable, most of them derived from contact with the wander-ing gipsies. He knows something of Romany, and speaks of the 'Diddikai', as he correctly calls him, or half-bred gipsy, as more dangerous and fierce than the rest. David, the old poacher and soldier, 'traveller' once, perchance, is keen-witted and thoughtful; at times a light smile plays gracefully about the wrinkles of time and trouble in his cheek. At night, when he gathers his boys about him, there is grave talk and bandied jest, and thrusts of wit. Perhaps in the midst of the 'godship' one is ailing, and inevitably he suffers doctoring with long, dark, bitter draughts of mysterious tea.

Cloud Castle

Lob

At hawthorn-time in Wiltshire travelling
In search of something chance would never bring,
An old man's face, by life and weather cut
And coloured—rough, brown, sweet as any nut,—
A land face, sea-blue-eyed—hung in my mind
When I had left him many a mile behind.

All he said was: 'Nobody can't stop 'ee. It's
A footpath, right enough. You see those bits
Of mounds—that's where they opened up the barrows
Sixty years since, while I was scaring sparrows.
They thought as there was something to find there,
But couldn't find it, by digging, anywhere.'

To turn back then and seek him, where was the use?
There were three Manningfords,—Abbots, Bohun, and Bruce:
And whether Alton, not Manningford, it was,
My memory could not decide, because
There was both Alton Barnes and Alton Priors.
All had their churches, graveyards, farms, and byres,
Lurking to one side up the paths and lanes,
Seldom well seen except by aeroplanes;
And when bells rang, or pigs squealed, or cocks crowed,
Then only heard. Ages ago the road
Approached. The people stood and looked and turned.
Nor asked it to come nearer, nor yet learned
To move out there and dwell in all men's dust.
And yet withal they shot the weathercock, just
Because 'twas he crowed out of tune, they said:
So now the copper weathercock is dead.
If they had reaped their dandelions and sold
Them fairly, they could have afforded gold.

Many years passed, and I went back again
Among those villages, and looked for men
Who might have known my ancient. He himself
Had long been dead or laid upon the shelf,
I thought. One man I asked about him roared
At my description: ''Tis old Bottlesford
He means, Bill.' But another said: 'Of course,
It was Jack Button up at the White Horse.
He's dead, sir, these three years.' This lasted till
A girl proposed Walker of Walker's Hill,
'Old Adam Walker. Adam's Point you'll see
Marked on the maps.'

'That was her roguery,'
The next man said. He was a squire's son
Who loved wild bird and beast, and dog and gun
For killing them. He had loved them from his birth,
One with another, as he loved the earth.
'The man may be like Button, or Walker, or
Like Bottlesford, that you want, but far more
He sounds like one I saw when I was a child.
I could almost swear to him. The man was wild
And wandered. His home was where he was free.
Everybody has met one such man as he.
Does he keep clear old paths that no one uses
But once a lifetime when he loves or muses?
He is English as this gate, these flowers, this mire.
And when at eight years old Lob-lie-by-the-fire
Came in my books, this was the man I saw.
He has been in England as long as dove and daw,
Calling the wild cherry tree the merry tree,
The rose campion Bridget-in-her-bravery;
And in a tender mood he, as I guess,
Christened one flower Love-in-idleness,
And while he walked from Exeter to Leeds
One April called all cuckoo-flowers Milkmaids.
From him old herbal Gerard learnt, as a boy,
To name wild clematis the Traveller's-joy.
Our blackbirds sang no English till his ear
Told him they called his Jan Toy 'Pretty dear'.
(She was Jan Toy the Lucky, who, having lost
A shilling, and found a penny loaf, rejoiced.)
For reasons of his own to him the wren
Is Jenny Pooter. Before all other men
'Twas he first called the Hog's Back the Hog's Back.
That Mother Dunch's Buttocks should not lack
Their name was his care. He too could explain
Totteridge and Totterdown and Juggler's Lane:
He knows, if anyone. Why Tumbling Bay,
Inland in Kent, is called so, he might say.

'But little he says compared with what he does.
If ever a sage troubles him he will buzz
Like a beehive to conclude the tedious fray:
And the sage, who knows all languages, runs away.
Yet Lob has thirteen hundred names for a fool,
And though he never could spare time for school
To unteach what the fox so well expressed,
On biting the cock's head off,—Quietness is best,—
He can talk quite as well as anyone
After his thinking is forgot and done.
He first of all told someone else's wife,
For a farthing she'd skin a flint and spoil a knife
Worth sixpence skinning it. She heard him speak:
"She had a face as long as a wet week"
Said he, telling the tale in after years.
With blue smock and with gold rings in his ears,
Sometimes he is a pedlar, not too poor
To keep his wit. This is tall Tom that bore
The logs in, and with Shakespeare in the hall
Once talked, when icicles hung by the wall.
As Herne the Hunter he has known hard times.
On sleepless nights he made up weather rhymes
Which others spoilt. And, Hob being then his name,
He kept the hog that thought the butcher came
To bring his breakfast. "You thought wrong," said Hob.
When there were kings in Kent this very Lob,
Whose sheep grew fat and he himself grew merry,
Wedded the king's daughter of Canterbury;
For he alone, unlike squire, lord, and king,
Watched a night by her without slumbering;
He kept both waking. When he was but a lad
He won a rich man's heiress, deaf, dumb, and sad,
By rousing her to laugh at him. He carried
His donkey on his back. So they were married.
And while he was a little cobbler's boy
He tricked the giant coming to destroy
Shrewsbury by flood. "And how far is it yet?"
The giant asked in passing. "I forget;
But see these shoes I've worn out on the road

And we're not there yet." He emptied out his load
Of shoes for mending. The giant let fall from his spade
The earth for damming Severn, and thus made
The Wrekin hill; and little Ercall hill
Rose where the giant scraped his boots. While still
So young, our Jack was chief of Gotham's sages.
But long before he could have been wise, ages
Earlier than this, while he grew thick and strong
And ate his bacon, or, at times, sang a song
And merely smelt it, as Jack the giant-killer
He made a name. He too ground up the miller,
The Yorkshireman who ground men's bones for flour.

'Do you believe Jack dead before his hour?
Or that his name is Walker, or Bottlesford,
Or Button, a mere clown, or squire, or lord?
The man you saw—Lob-lie-by-the-fire, Jack Cade,
Jack Smith, Jack Moon, poor Jack of every trade,
Young Jack, or old Jack, or Jack What-d'ye-call
Jack-in-the-hedge, or Robin-run-by-the-wall,
Robin Hood, Ragged Robin, lazy Bob,
One of the lords of No Man's Land, good Lob,—
Although he was seen dying at Waterloo,
Hastings, Agincourt, and Sedgemoor too,—
Lives yet. He never will admit he is dead
Till millers cease to grind men's bones for bread,
Not till our weathercock crows once again
And I remove my house out of the lane
On to the road.' With this he disappeared
In hazel and thorn tangled with old-man's-beard.
But one glimpse of his back, as there he stood,
Choosing his way, proved him of old Jack's blood,
Young Jack perhaps, and now a Wiltshireman
As he has oft been since his days began.

Collected Poems

An Old Couple

Their house is a small russet cave of three dim compartments—part of
a farmhouse, the rest having fallen to ruin, and from human hands to
the starlings, the sparrows, and the rats. No one will live in it again.
Inside, it is held together by the solid poetry of their lives, by gay-
coloured, cheerful, tradesmen's pictures of well-dressed children and
blooming horse-women, and the dogs of gentlemen, memorial cards
of the dead, a few photographs, some picture post-cards pasted over
flaws in the wall, and the worn furniture of several disconnected generations. The old man's tools in the kitchen are noble—the heavy wrought-
iron, two-toothed hoe, that falls pleasantly upon the hard clay and
splits it without effort and without jarring the hand, its ash handle
worn thin where his hand has glided at work, a hand that nothing will
wear smooth; the glittering, yellow-handled spades and forks; the
disused shovel with which he boasts regretfully that he could dig his
garden when he lived on deep loam in a richer country than this; and
still the useless 'hop-idgit' of six tynes—the Sussex 'shim'—which he
retains to remind others, and perhaps himself, that he was a farmer
once. He had twenty or thirty acres and a few cows. The cows all died
in one year and he became a labourer.

His wife remembers those days. She was a tall woman and stooped
at the doorway thatch; now she cannot rise to it. For every day she
went many times to the sweet brook, a quarter of a mile away, rather
than take the grey liquor of the pond for her cows. That is how she
came to be bent like an oak branch on which children swing, or like a
thorn that knows the west wind on the hill or the shore. Now she
cannot carry a pail, for it would sweep the ground. She cannot see the
apples in autumn until they have fallen to her feet. Her flesh seems to
have assumed an animal sweetness, for her bees will cluster on the
brown hands. Birds and beasts take to her as to an old tree, though she
has pity for them but no love. Sometimes as she sits at her door the
robins come fearlessly close to her—hedge-sparrows too, if there is
nobody else near, and even the partridges that come for the ants in the

old dock roots. She watches them with her dull eye and seems easily to have found a Franciscan friendliness when, as if angry with the creatures for seeing her frailty, she stamps her feet and drives them away. Then she relents and tries her power, as if she has half persuaded herself that it is a happy talent. She will crush a mouse in her fingers, and yet they still run over her in their merry business night or day, as they would over a tree that had fallen, and proved fatal to some of them in its death. Yet, in spite of her apparent indifference, I think that she knows the animals more than we who patronize them. Left alone with a cat, she shows, indeed, none of the endearments of a civilized woman, but quietly concedes and demands concessions, very much as when a horse and some cows are sheltering from the heat together in a limited shade.

Compared with Margaret Helen Page, her husband, Robert, is a citizen of the world. He knows all the farmers in the neighbourhood, thatching for one, haymaking for another, gardening, woodcutting, washing, or pole-pulling in the hop-garden for others. He can even make the beautiful, five-barred gates, with their noble top bars, tapered and shaped like a gunstock and barrel. All the inns are known to him, and the labourers and wayfaring men who resort to them. He will gossip, and the rich do not disdain to listen to the fabrications and selections which he mixes charmingly for them alone. The workhouse or death is not more than a few years ahead of him; for he stoops with difficulty and will make haste for no man; yet he will cheerfully quarrel with a farmer in the middle of the winter, pick up his coat, take his wages, and go off to the inn and drink all that he has; if the farmer grumbles in September that Robert has been taking merely an honest bushel of hops from the pickers, he will not give way to the extent of a handful. No one can thatch as he can. His tall haystacks look like churches when they are new, and so they remain. The roofs of his cornricks are shaped like breasts, with convex curves that make the same lines against the sky as you walk round. His vegetable plots are invariably as flat as lawns, their sides evenly sloping to the paths. He stops in the midst of his work and smokes and thinks; and he expects to be paid for his thinking. In the spring he catches moles, hanging them up on the briers or thorns with great care, twisting the twigs round them so that they stay until fur and bone are indistinguishable and break up into dust.

At the inns he hears the gossip of the universe, heaping up as in a marine store the details of murders, swindles, divorces, expensive pictures of Venus, etc., horse races, cricket matches, letters from archbishops and literary men, distant wars, new foods and diseases and cures, automobiles, the cost of rich men's dinners, how to live happily, the extravagance of the poor, how to feed on a shilling a week. These things are 'in print' and therefore true. But he utters no opinions of his own. He consents to exchange his recollections and to accept others; then he sinks into the happy silence of those who have not the gift of ratiocination. What dark, undisturbed depths of personality are his— immense depths yielding to the upper world, now and then, an ejaculation, as Gilbert White's well yielded a black lizard at times.

'I wonder,' he ejaculated once, 'I wonder what God did with himself before he made such a kettle of fish as this world.'

The Heart of England

The Landlord of the 'Cross Inn'

A very pretty companion for Jones was Owen, the innkeeper, a robust man of words, who called himself the preacher's best customer, because he needed so much of his charity.

He was a perfect Celt, according to the English superstition. For never was there such a failure who was also such a swaggerer as he. He had fair hair, blue eyes, and a small, elegant beard, which

Business could not make dull, nor passion wild.

He was bullied by a contemptuous wife; he was ridiculed by all his regular customers, rallied by the rest. But the beard was always neat and fair, a symbol of his unconquerable mind. No matter how he was trodden down, he smelt sweet. He had humour, for he could laugh at himself, though he lacked the common gift of being able to laugh at others, and had no repartee. The more lusty the Saturday night thrusts at him, the more vivid was his reply, and it was commonly a piece of egoism and self-exposure, which, if not so long and so wonderfully draped, would have called for a repetition of the very blow he was parrying. Once when he had been sold up and had little more than a wife and a walking-stick in the world, and his position attracted some trifling compliments and condolences from his old harriers, he stood up, and, wielding his stick and motioning to his wife to be silent, gave an inventory of the things he had lost with such decoration as would have abashed an auctioneer. There is a Welsh proverb, 'A Welshman keeps nothing until he has lost it'; and the now invisible and inaccessible furniture called up such a tumult of admiration that he cared not that it was no longer his. How rich he looked! As the words flowed on and it was time for his hearers to be going, it was clear that if he had forgotten anything, he had invented more; but though he ended in no better company than that of his wife, who picked something from his coat and held it between the tips of two fingers for his humiliation, he but wiped his forehead and cursed because he had forgotten the ancient horse-trappings of brass that used to hang over the mantelpiece at the —— Arms.

His voice, whether he sang or spoke, was of wide range and exquisite adjustment, and he spoke with care and gusto, as if he loved his native tongue. Under its influence, he respected nobody of any importance. Thus, he was once pretty justly thrashed; when, having tired his chastiser by his patience, he remarked at great length that he supposed the other did not know who he was, and the splendour of his manner overcame his heated companion. No sooner had he got home than he gave a rapturous description of how one had given another a thrashing down the road. He did it so well that he was asked whether he was the beater. 'No,' said he bravely, 'it happened that I was beat.'

Had he lost by a bargain, had he taken a bad coin unawares, had he been worsted in argument, he could so rant that he moved every one, and himself obviously first of all, and made the worse appear the better. He kept a genealogical tree in constant use by pruning and watering, and though there was not only a prince but a poet in it, I think he gloried less in the old splendour of his family than in the length of its fall, as who should say he had once been so high that he was 'from morn to dewy eve' in falling.

When first I saw him, he had just come into the 'Cross Inn'. It was midday; the weather was cold and wet; and since he never liked to see a man drinking by himself, and the shepherds coming down from the mountains to market had called pretty often, he was not sober. He told me that his was a fine house—the finest in the village, and therefore in the county; and that it had not paid the former tenant well, who had, in fact, sold but eighteen gallons of beer in a month. He was going to do better than that, he said; to make a beginning, he was going to drink that quantity himself. I asked for brandy. He had not a drop, and explained that he had a weakness for it himself—took a drop very often; and that therefore, to get out of temptation, he had finished his stock on the night before. 'But,' said he, 'I have upstairs such a bed as you—pardon me—never slept in yet.'

'I have no doubt,' said I, and sat down.

But when he heard that I was walking across Wales, and had therefore tried many beds, he insisted that I should see the thing. It was the finest in the village—in the county—in Wales—'I don't see why I should not say in the whole world.' Truly it was a noble bed, in a great, empty, raftered, uncarpeted room; the wood all darkened oak, with a dusky gleam; the hangings ample and of a rich crimson stuff; the purity of the linen splendid. If a royal person or a poet had not slept in it, 'that was their misfortune.' He stood by, awed and reverent, beholding the bed. I was not his equal in eloquence, and he echoed my praise with an elaborate 'of course': and for the sake of hearing some of the words he loved, he finally invited me to spend a night in the bed, 'as his guest,' so he magnificently said.

All his family were of the same temper. His father and mother had gone to London years ago, and, at seventy years of age, to the infirmary of a workhouse. . . .

The aged paupers sat in a long, grey, motionless, and silent row—like a sculptured frieze, or like persons expecting to be photographed —under the wall of a church. Before them was a strip of grass, one emerald half of which shone so that it seemed of an element like flame; for it was pure, insubstantial colour; and into this, as the paupers saw, the tide of the shadow of the church gradually ate. Beyond the grass was the infirmary, and alongside it a yellow road, and on that a hearse. Watching this and the paupers, a crowd of persons, with uninterested, inquisitive eyes and bowler hats, stuck their noses through the railings which ran between the busy street and the infirmary. Motor cars brayed, hooves clattered.

Presently three men carried out a coffin, containing the remains of Mrs. Owen, and shoved it into the hearse. 'God love me, what a coffin!' said one of the crowd. But the frieze of paupers were silent and motionless in the long grey row—all but the husband of the corpse. He, like the others, seemed to stare at the hearse with fixed gaze, and in a loud voice he remembered what a bonny woman the corpse had been, and in particular how, while a travelling musician played in the village street, when she was past fifty years of age, she had locked herself into the kitchen and danced, having spread a mat to deaden the clicking of her merry clogs; and he had watched her, unobserved. The story and his uncontrolled, bleating voice raised a laugh under the bowler hats; and the old men lifted their heads and straightened themselves and laughed; and most loudly and grimly of all laughed Owen, while he remembered the cottage in sight of the beacons of Breconshire; and the hearse rolled out and the crowd removed.

Wales

Head and Bottle

The downs will lose the sun, white alyssum
Lose the bees' hum;
But head and bottle tilted back in the cart
Will never part
Till I am cold as midnight and all my hours
Are beeless flowers.
He neither sees, nor hears, nor smells, nor thinks,
But only drinks,
Quiet in the yard where tree trunks do not lie
More quietly.

Collected Poems

Milking

The end of April was sappy, careless, and profuse. One day it was all eagerness and energy and gave no rest to the wind and the sun, on the earth or in the waters or in the clouds of the sky, and the songs of the birds were a mad medley. Another day it was indolent: a soft grey sky without form covered all; there was no wind; the birds were still; the lusty, buxom spring, a pretty and merry slut, with her sleeves and skirts tucked up and her hair down over her eyes and shoulders, had fallen asleep in the midst of her toil and nothing could waken her but a thunderstorm in the night. The next day she was simply at play with showers and sunlight, sunlight and showers, at play with sky and earth as if they were but coloured silks and now she fluttered the white and blue and green together and then, wearying of that, held up the grey and the grey-white and the green, and lastly mingled all together inextricably. For the most part she preferred not to let either go quite out of sight; when the heavy rain fell on the rustling wood it was out of a sky serene, lustrous, and mild; and when the light was steady and the rain tripping away from it upon myriad feet down among the leaves to the earth, still the shadows of the rain clouds stole over the hills like smoke. There was a gamesome spirit abroad. It was seen in the amorous conflict of rain and sun, and heard in the cry of the titmouse along the hedge: 'Fitchy! fitchy!'

Rain or not, always far away in the south there was a cluster of white peaks apparently belonging to a land that knew neither our sun nor our rain. Rain or sunshine or both made little difference to the shed at the cross roads. It was shadowy and old under a roof that was patched and hollowed like the sail of a ship. The door was open, but on either side the piles of dung were high and long and allowed the sun to enter the shed only for half an hour each day. And now in that half-hour the farmer Weekes was going to milk the last of his seven cows. Until now he had known of the afternoon only that the wind whined in the roof and that the rain dripped through on to his back at intervals. When the sun at last stepped in between the banks of dung he could see that it was a forward spring. For his eye travelled up between the green walls of the road to the hills four miles away, and there the beech trees were almost in perfect leaf and in their dense ranks resembled a flock of sheep with golden fleeces descending the slope. Yet it wanted a week before May-day. The grass was good, and already the cows were clean and bright after their winter in the yard; and, having looked at his hands alongside the white and strawberry hide of the cow, he got up and wiped them on a wisp of grass beside the door. He stood there a moment—a tall, crooked man, with ever-sparkling eyes in a nubbly and bony head, worn down by sun and toil and calamity to nothing but a stone, hollowed and grey, to which his short black hair clung like moss; in his starved fields you might have found a weathered flint of the same shape, and have said that it was much like a man's head. He stretched himself, and then turned and called the cow by her name in a voice so deep and powerful that it was as if the whole shed and not a man's chest had uttered it.

He sat down again to milk and to think, with his face turned to the sun. He was thinking of the farmhouse under those woods on the hill, where he used to go courting twenty years ago, and of the girl, the only daughter of that house, who was now his wife. He had driven over there one day in his father's cart to see about some pigs. The old man had given him supper, honey and bread and butter, cold apple dumplings with cheese, and cowslip wine. It was a wonderful quiet house, very dark under tall beeches, with a quality in the dark still air as if it were under water, but very clean and bright with china and brass and the white tablecloth and the old man's white beard and glittering blue eyes. He knew that the old man was failing to make both ends meet, but there was no sign of it, and he spoke with a cheerful gravity, and there was a look about house and man as if they were apart from the world, and not subject to such accidents as failure of crops, cattle disease, and the like. They had done their business, and at the end of a long silence he was thinking of rising to go, when Emily, the daughter, came in without noticing him, kissed her father, and said, 'Father, there is a white bird in the old apple tree of the rickyard singing like a blackbird. Yet 'tis as white as milk.'

'Well, we will all come and see,' said the old man, and then she saw that a stranger was there, and with a blush she retreated and opened the door. As she was shutting it she turned round out of curiosity, thus revealing her own face to the stranger, but seeing nothing of his which was in shadow. In a minute or two they went out into the rickyard where the cart was waiting. Emily was patting the horse's neck, but with her face towards the old apple-tree where a white blackbird was singing from the topmost branch. 'You will not let them shoot it, father, will you?' she said. The white bird and its song, the girl's fair hair, and rosy face very serious, the unbent old man soon to die, the sombre smouldering old tiles and brick wall of the house, and the high black woods behind, were remembered now. Soon afterwards he had returned to the house, and again and again, avowedly to see Emily. In the late summer they used to walk out after the haymaking was all over, while the night-jar sang and the woods were dark and discreet and the sky above them as pale green as a new-mown field. They went in amongst the untrodden bracken together. He could recall the smell of the crushed fronds where they sat, the light of the near planet between the fox-gloves gushing from the violet sky, and the kisses that were as sweet as the honeysuckle overhanging them, and, unlike that, could be tasted again and again without cloying.

And now the cold whine of the wind in the roof and the drop of the rain, and Emily was lying at home, sick, with a dead newborn child in the next room, and a child that he was glad was dead, yes! that even she would not be crying after if she knew what a monstrous mistaken thing had come into the world with their help. Weekes looked at that old farmhouse and the rickyard, the crushed bracken bower, as if to search among these things engraved by joy upon his brain for the devilish magic that had brought about this wretchedness. He looked at her remembered face, scanning it for something to explain this thing, looked closely and fiercely at the face that was turned back towards him in her father's doorway so that he loved her from that day. What? Why? But neither in the young girl nor in the worn woman could he see what he sought. He thought of their labours, of the six children she had borne and reared, of her rough hands and wrenched voice, of the smearing out of all her prettiness except her hair. He turned it over and over, ruminating, undisturbed by the spurting of the milk into the pail, the trickle of the shower, or the sight of the hills and the clouds over the hills. Yet he did not take his eyes off these hills, nor change the look given to them by his pain and questioning—questioning he knew not what now—the whole order of things, perhaps, from which the terror had sprung unexpected. Having naught for his brain to grip and hold, but only the dead ghastly child lying still, and repeating the question, and round about it the moving world of men and Nature, enormous and endless and careless, each effort was weaker than the last and sorrow brought its narcotic stupidity. It was some time after he had drawn her last milk that the cow licked his face impatiently. He kicked away the stool and began singing a verse of a ribald song which he did not know he had remembered—

> *Poor Sally's face is plain*
> *But Sally's heart is kind—*

And it was so singing that, without wishing it, he returned the question to the teeming womb and grave of the earth, to be swallowed up in the vast profusion of life and death, while the merry maid waved to and fro the coloured silks of the sunshine and of the rain, and the titmouse crept through the hedge, crying, waggishly, 'Fitchy! fitchy!'

Rest and Unrest

The Ploughman

Richard the ploughman is worthy of his plough and team. He moves heavily with long strides over the baked yellow field, swaying with the violent motion of the plough as it cuts the stubborn and knotty soil, and yet seeming to sway out of joy and not necessity. He is a straight, small-featured, thin-lipped man, red-haired and with blue eyes of a fierce loneliness almost fanatical. Hour after hour he crosses and re-crosses the field, up to the ridge, whence he can see miles of hill and wood; down to the woodside where the rabbits hardly trouble to hide as he appears, or to the thick hedge with marigolds below and nearly all day the song of nightingales. The furrow is always straight; he could plough it so asleep, and sometimes perhaps he does. The larks sing invisible in the white May sky. The swallows and woodlarks and willow-wrens and linnets, with their tenderest of all mortal voices, flit and sing about him. Partridges whirr and twang. A fox steals along the hedge, a squirrel glows and ripples across a bay of the field. And for a little time he notices these things in a mild complacency. He has even formed a theory that there is another finch like a chaffinch, but not such a singer, and he calls it a piefinch. He likes the bright weather, and his cheerful greeting leaves the passer-by feeling stupid because he cannot equal it; few sounds can equal it, except the shout of a cuckoo and the abandoned clamour of a deep-voiced hound. He never becomes tired; at noon and evening in the tavern, he drinks standing, with one hand on the high door latch and the other holding the tankard, and talking all the time at the rate of one phrase to a minute, with serious mouth and distant eyes which must be symbols to help out the words, for certainly if those words mean no more than they would in another man's mouth, they convey little but the apparent ennui of all those long hours walking to this oak or that hawthorn spray.

At first sight the ploughman's task seems to be one which ought rightly to be set only to some well-balanced philosopher, who could calmly descend into himself during the many lonely hours and think of nature and man in orderly thoughts. To the ordinary man, with his drug-habit of taking to reverie during any long spell of solitude, such a task would seem fatal. In fact, it is pretty certain that many a plain fellow must be turned into a fool by the immense monotony of similar furrows and the same view repeated exactly every quarter of an hour. When he is still a boy, he goes about, even in the four hours' darkness of the winter mornings, with always a song amidst the sleet or the silent frost. At lunch he can look for nests or nuts or hunt a stoat. When work is over he looks forward to songs at 'The Chequers' with those of his own age, or to a shame-faced walk with a girl, or to fishing for tench and eels, or even to a game of cricket. But when he is married all that is past. He leads his horses down to the plough, having some simple thought, a grievance, a recollection, perhaps a hope, running confusedly in his head, and all day he turns it over, repeating himself, exaggerating, puzzling over the meaning of someone's words, floundering in digressions, fitting new words to the wood-pigeon's talk, trying to keep straight and to make up his mind, justifying himself, condemning another, cursing him. Now and then he lifts his eyes to the sky or the wooded hills and his mind catches at an impression which never becomes a thought, but something between a picture and a tune in the head, and its half-oblivion is pleasant, when suddenly the plough leaps forward from his relaxing grasp, he shouts 'Ah, Charley!' to the leader, mutters a little, and settles down again to the grievance or the recollection or the hope, to be disturbed on lucky days by the hounds, perhaps, but otherwise to go on and on; and at noon and evening he takes his horses back to the stable and confronts men with the same simple ejaculations as before, after the last glass possibly reviving his lonely thoughts, but ineffectually. 'How Bill does talk,' they say. What wonder that the rustic moralist marks an infant's tomb with the words:

> *When the archangel trump shall blow*
> *And souls to body join,*
> *Millions shall wish their lives below*
> *Had been as bright as thine.*

But Richard is no ordinary man, for he is happy and proud, and somewhere in the fields or in the clouds that roll before him as his plough comes to the top of the ridge, he has found that draught of excellent grace:

Few men but such as sober are and sage,
Are by the gods to drink thereof assigned;
But such as drink, eternal happiness to find.

There is little of wisdom in his words except moderation; but his garden is luckier, his kitchen sweeter than all the rest in the hamlet, and of all his tasks—ploughing, harrowing, rolling, drudging, reaping, mowing, carting faggots or corn or hay or green meat or dung—he likes none better than the others, because he likes them all well as they come. And ah! to see him and his team all dark and large and heroic against the sky, ploughing in the winter or the summer morning, or to see him grooming the radiant horses in their dim stable on a calm, delaying evening, is to see one who is in league with sun and wind and rain to make odours fume richly from the ancient altar, to keep the earth going in beauty and fruitfulness for still more years.

The Heart of England

As the Team's Head-Brass

As the team's head-brass flashed out on the turn
The lovers disappeared into the wood.
I sat among the boughs of the fallen elm
That strewed the angle of the fallow, and
Watched the plough narrowing a yellow square
Of charlock. Every time the horses turned
Instead of treading me down, the ploughman leaned
Upon the handles to say or ask a word,
About the weather, next about the war.
Scraping the share he faced towards the wood,
And screwed along the furrow till the brass flashed
Once more.
            The blizzard felled the elm whose crest
I sat in, by a woodpecker's round hole,
The ploughman said, 'When will they take it away?'
'When the war's over.' So the talk began—
One minute and an interval of ten,

A minute more and the same interval.
'Have you been out?' 'No.' 'And don't want to,
    perhaps?'
'If I could only come back again, I should.
I could spare an arm. I shouldn't want to lose
A leg. If I should lose my head, why, so,
I should want nothing more. . . . Have many gone
From here?' 'Yes.' 'Many lost?' 'Yes, a good few.
Only two teams work on the farm this year.
One of my mates is dead. The second day
In France they killed him. It was back in March,
The very night of the blizzard, too. Now if
He had stayed here we should have moved the tree.'
'And I should not have sat here. Everything
Would have been different. For it would have been
Another world.' 'Ay, and a better, though
If we could see all all might seem good.' Then
The lovers came out of the wood again:
The horses started and for the last time
I watched the clods crumble and topple over
After the ploughshare and the stumbling team.

Collected Poems

THROUGH
THE YEAR

E

A Touch of Winter

All around a light fall of snow has checkered the meadows and the ploughlands of the valley with fleecy white, like cirrus clouds that fleck the azure sky. It lies thickest in the hollows and on the footways; in the shelter of the tall hedges it has drifted deep. Looking only at the exposed fields, the aspect is wintry; but in strange contrast are the hedge-mounds that line the road and border the copses. The summer verdure, indeed, is gone—red-robin, knapweed, even herb Robert and the grasses, are withered and hidden by the drifted leaves. Yet everywhere are scattered signs that we look for only in spring. Succulent shoots of many plants peep through the dropped leaves out of the cold earth. Deeply lobed foliage of celandine springs in plenty by the ditch side, and with it palest green of ground-ivy—hardly seen, so small and delicate are the leaves. Chickweed in masses, spangled with little starry flowers, has sprung up—unnoticed till it has put out its many blossoms. But commonest of all, and most beautiful with its whorled leaves trailing about the mound and leaning over the lowermost hawthorn-twigs, is the goose grass, well known for its habit of attaching itself to the clothing. To the rustic it is known as 'clytes'; and the tiny berries, that adhere even more readily than the foliage, are called 'sweethearts'. Not yet long enough to festoon the hedge as in summer, the stems shoot up several inches high, pale as the young ground-ivy. Nettles, shorter still, and only recently emerged from the ground, rise here and there in small clusters. More vigorous than any in its spreading growth is the hedge-parsley, with its intricately-cut leaves. Here also a haw has fallen, and, buried beneath the leaves, has sprouted forth and sent up a slender red shoot adorned with spring-green leaves: in the same manner young seedling elms, no taller than the nettles, have grown up under this cold sky and biting wind. Many another plant, such as the broad dock and wild parsnip, has burst into leaf about this same hedge.

Alongside the road, but some yards apart, runs a deep wide ditch, resembling a west country lane. Through a grove of beech and ash it

goes, and underfoot their leaves lie rotting many inches thick. Bushes of
bramble and elder straggle across the way, and in places knotted roots,
raised high above the earth, render the walking difficult. Though
parted from the road only by a strip of sward grown with young
beeches, it is utterly shut out from the highway, busy with market-
carts. Hither flock the titmice, scared from the more frequented path,
and the blackbirds come to pull a worm from the moist earth. Among
the boughs scatter the merry great tits, and away into the underwood.
Close at hand two robins flit in the dense cover of the thorns, recalling
by their motions the amorous chasing of late February days. Afar in
the turnips or the oat-stubble we can hear at intervals the cry of
partridges. Overhead, now and again, fly the banded larks bound for
new feeding-grounds. Tall burdocks rise up frequently in the ditch
with their bristling clusters, and about the mounds on either hand dark
shining ivy creeps, rounding off the rugged banks. Now the hollow
widens out till it is lost in an underwood of blackthorns; but beyond it
is steep-sided and narrow once more. In the crooked limbs of oak that
roof the grassy ditch blue-tits call loudly as they scatter. Screened from
the blast, all the young green growths may be seen that flourished on
the hedgemounds behind. Where this sheltered hollow ends, almost at
a farmhouse door, a great yew-tree leans over, and in its dense stiff
foliage the wind makes moan like a sea lapping on the shingle. Fresh
twigs cluster thickly about the old peeling stem, and, with the darker
leaves, appear to be varnished, so glossy are they. The smaller branches
of the oaks are tinged with a ruddy hue like willow-wands.

From some point not far distant comes a song that is rarely heard in
December. These sweet though melancholy notes are unmistakeably
the chaffinch's. We are disappointed to find the handsome pink-
breasted bird prisoned in a cage hanging against the farmstead wall. On
the ancient bricks so dull and brown the yellow blossoms of the jasmine
are studded thick, and they creep on to the tiled roof, weather-stained
to browns and dingy reds. Most of the flint cottage walls along the
road are flaming with the same bright-blossoming creeper.

Passing the farmyard and the pied pigeons fluttering among the
horses' feet, the road itself is worn deep through sand and chalk. So
tall on each side is the wall of crumbling earth we cannot see the
meadows above, and the elms that stand away from the track. Just over
the sand a thin stratum of dark loam, bound together as it were by the
many rootlets that stretch hither, juts beetling out towards the road-

way; and hanging from this rich dark layer a waving rootlet of elder has sprouted afresh into leaf, though several inches away from the low cliff of sand.

At length the road emerges from its groove on to the hill-top, and once more it is level and bounded by narrow woods of spruce, whence comes the startling challenge of the pheasant-cocks. Meanwhile the twilight air has become keener and the wind rises—humming through the green firs. The smaller birds are nearly all in cover, and only a belated pipit or a steady flapping rook moves aloft in the rude air. Sometimes, in the hedges that line the way, robins rustle gently and fly a yard or two, or a blackbird blusters out; otherwise the life so lately stirring is silent, and the tomtits are rocked asleep amid the swaying larch-boughs. Out in the fields, freshly turned by the plough, peewits run rapidly hither and thither, occasionally chirruping a low distressful note, unlike their usual screaming wail. The whole flock is within thirty yards of us, and their markings are perfectly clear—the flowing crest, the dark band beneath the throat, and the snow-white breast, showing against the clods. With the chilling wind the snow begins to fall again, and from the shelter of this holly-tree we can watch the flakes drifting swiftly across the meadows, and rolling like thin smoke, silvering the sward and heaping by the ditches. Still the peewits move uneasily in the open, always facing the wind and the thin wall of snow bearing down upon them. Scared by a sportsman passing near them, several rise, but soon settle again, running a short distance in the very teeth of the blast. Some of them stand huddled in the furrows, as partridges do by the ant-hillocks. At length the snow ceases and the wind drops to a whisper; then over the hill-top the lapwings start up again and wheel in phantom flight, shrieking their weird night call.

The Woodland Life

Snow

The colour of the dawn is lead and white—white snow falling out of a leaden sky to the white earth. The rose branches bend in sharper and sharper curves to the ground, the loaded yew sprays sweep the snow with white plumes. On the sedges the snow is in fleeces; the light strands of clematis are without motion, and have gathered it in clots.

One thrush sings, but cannot long endure the sound of his un-challenged note; the sparrows chirrup in the ricks; the blackbird is waiting for the end of that low tingling noise of the snow falling straight in windless air.

At mid-day the snow is finer, and almost rain, and it begins to pour down from its hives among the branches in short showers or in heavy hovering lumps. The leaves of ivy and holly are gradually exposed in all their gloomy polish, and out bursts the purple of the ash buds and the yellow of new foliage. The beech stems seem in their wetness to be made of a dark agate. Out from their tops blow rags of mist, and not far above them clouds like old spiders' webs go rapidly by.

The snow falls again and the voices of the little summer birds are buried in the silence of the flakes that whirl this way and that aimlessly, rising and falling and crossing or darting horizontally, making the trees sway wearily and their light tops toss and their numbers roar continually in the legions of the wind that whine and moan and shriek their hearts out in the solitary house roofs and doors and round about. The silence of snow co-exists with this roar. One wren pierces it with a needle of song and is gone. The earth and sky are drowning in night and snow.

The South Country

January

It is January, and the predominant grass is green and shining in the sun. The rusty oaks and the farmhouse roofs glow. The bare clean hedges glitter with all their stems of olive hazel, silver oak and ash and whitethorn, and blackthorn ruddy where the cattle have rubbed. A lark rises and sings. A flock of linnets scatters and drops little notes like a rain of singing dew, and over all is a high blue sky, across which the west wind sets a fleet of bright white clouds to sail: into this blue sky the woods of the horizon drive their black teeth.

In the immense crystal spaces of fine windy air thus bounded by blue sky, black woods, and green grass, the jackdaws play. They soar, they float, they dance, and they dive and carve sudden magnificent precipices in the air, crying all the time with sharp, joyous cries that are in harmony with the great heights and the dashing wind. The carter's boy raises his head from the furrow and shouts to them now and then, while the brass furnishings of his horses gleam, their shoulders grow proud and their black tails stream out above the blue furrow and the silver plough.

Suddenly a pheasant is hurled out of a neighbouring copse; something crosses the road; and out over a large and shining meadow goes a fox, tall and red, going easily as if he sailed in the wind. He crosses that meadow, then another, and he is half a mile away before a loud halloo sounds in the third field, and a mile away before the first hound crosses the road upon his scent.

Run hard, hounds, and drown the jackdaws' calling with your concerted voices. It is good to see your long swift train across the meadow and away, away; on such a day a man would give everything to run like that. Run hard, fox, and may you escape, for it would not be well to die on such a day, unless you could perchance first set your fair teeth into the throats of the foolish ones who now break through the hedge on great horses and pursue you—I know not why—ignorant of the command that has gone forth from the heart of this high blue heaven, Be beautiful and enjoy and live!

The Heart of England

February Afternoon

Men heard this roar of parleying starlings, saw,
   A thousand years ago even as now,
   Black rooks with white gulls following the plough
So that the first are last until a caw
Commands that last are first again,—a law
   Which was of old when one, like me, dreamed how
   A thousand years might dust lie on his brow
Yet thus would birds do between hedge and shaw.

Time swims before me, making as a day
   A thousand years, while the broad ploughland oak
   Roars mill-like and men strike and bear the stroke

Of war as ever, audacious or resigned,
And God still sits aloft in the array
That we have wrought him, stone-deaf and stone-blind.

Collected Poems

Flowers of Frost

When winter is over and gone, we are often unjust to it and inclined to regard it as a kind of uniform white egg out of which the beautiful many-coloured spring was born. But the variety which we smooth away from our memories in order to produce this conventional picture of winter is really all but equal to that of spring. Frosts are superficially monotonous enough, but out of a score of frosts few are conceived and executed in the same way. There are typical frosty nights followed by typical frosty days, and the number of these overpowers the exceptions. And it is true that these nights are often majestic, so that I wonder more people do not deliberately watch the action of the great and infinitely varied dramas of night as they watch mountains or seas. There is one such typical night, for example, which is born from a candied violet sky in the twilight without any wind. A huge edifice of sombre cloud lingers late in the south-west, crumbles gradually away and leaves a pale blue that lasts nearly till dawn. The full night is clear and still. You can count the stars, but those few are intensely bright and seem to drip with moist splendour. All is silent except for five minutes when two dog-foxes meet in a glade, and while they fight scream as wildly as cats and in similar tones, but less shrill and more malignant; the victor goes barking wearily away. Then from the north-west clouds begin to ascend, and before you are aware have covered all the sky with grey that is broken up like sun-baked mud, with watery light in the interstices: and presently the sun is seen well above the horizon, bright but with a confined radiance, so that it stains only the nearest of the dark clouds, on which it rests like a gold crown on a bier. The misselthrushes, foreseeing thaw, sing in the shadowed beeches, up to which sweep the long undulations of pasture white with frost but without a glitter.

Far more uncommon is the night that pours down violent rain every now and then from among its many unclouded stars. Thunder approaches on lumbering wheels and is hardly believed in before the peals are drowning the roar of the gale in the trees and the flashes are awakening the pheasant cocks. The artillery draws off as if it had been the lightest and swiftest of cavalry, and the sky is lucid and serene. The end of the night is still, and the frost steals upon the world like moonlight from underground. No bird sings; only five or six goldfinches twitter as they flit round the heads of rigid teazels on the waste. The frost is to last, and before the sun sets the yellow menace of snow will have settled down over the earth and blotted out the Downs, which could be seen for fifty miles in the dawn. The hoar powder changes even the beauty of the familiar trees into something that never becomes a matter of course. The beeches that were yesterday a brood of giantesses are now insubstantial and as delicate as flowers of grass. The frost has been heavy, and the fields between the road and the woods are pure white without a seam. No footmark has touched the solitude, and it looks as if no one ever would cross it and enter the dark wood that is guarded so fairly. Nowhere is this inviolate look of the frosted woods more memorable than on the outskirts of London when the lamps on an open road are still glimmering and men are hurrying towards their trains. At the verge of the wood the haggard grey and drab umbelliferous plants are flowering again with crystal flowers. Inside the wood the frost has played at other mockeries. Each fragment of chalk is capped with ice, usually resembling a tooth, which is sometimes more than an inch long, and either perpendicular or slightly hooked at the tapering tip. The earth under the beeches has almost been covered by moss and ivy, and they have not been reached by the frost; yet here and there in the wood there is a gleam in those dark leaves as white as a dewy mushroom. Lying over the ivy is what might be the distaff, hastily thrown aside, from which the Fates were spinning the thread of some singularly fortunate, pure life—a distaff as it were bound round the middle with whitest wool. The distaff is a rotten peeling branch of beech, and the wool is a frost flower, such as may be found on any frosty, still day and always attached to a branch like this. The frost looks as if it had grown out of the dead wood; it is white and glossy, and curled like the under-wool which the shearer exposes on the belly of a sheep when he begins to shear it for the first time; but it is finer than any wool, and the threads, as much as three inches long, are all distinct as if combed. On some branches there are more than one, and of these one may be a large handful and another no bigger than the curl of a new-born child. Often the same stick will be singled out day after day for this exquisite attention from the frost.

Of a different kind is the beauty of the blades of ice that will occasionally be found attached to one side, not necessarily the under side, of every twig on every tree in the wood, and to every dead stem of dock and ragwort in the neglected fields above. These blades, having an even or a serrated edge and either as clear as glass or powdered with hoar frost, reach a breadth of an inch or more and almost the thickness of a sword. When it thaws they fall in rustling, jingling, glittering showers, and lie on the earth in fragments that soon melt together into mounds of a tender grey.

There is never any lack of colour in the woods of winter and the wooded hillsides; but frost is the discoverer of some of the most delicate harmonies. For example, the tender green, silvered green and willow grey of the juniper foliage, the white of melting frost, the harder white of the rime where the shadows of the bushes preserve it from the sun, and the other white which looks pale blue against the dark green of yew trees. And, again, in an old marl-pit against the side of a hill you will often meet the harmony of clear white frost, the grey or drab white of the fraying marl itself, the softer and darker cygnet colour of the old traveller's joy floating above and about the hazel bushes at the foot of the cliff, the grey mud of the cart-ruts, the still darker shades in the bark and the crisp fallen leaves of white-beam below, while perhaps a cloud will rise out of the blue sky above and add the white of sunlit marble, or the rose drift after dawn will be reflected in the whites beneath it, or the vapour from some warmer spot will float over and hang and swirl and spread banner-like among the beeches at the side. Another notable harmony is made by the seashore when the moors are dappled and the sands white with frost, the tall waves foam-crested, the sky milky blue and pierced only by the morning star. There is a harmony of colour and sound between the frost on the mountains and the curlew's cry. Beautiful are the rough ploughlands whose clods and ridges hold the frost and form a chequer which is repeated by the hard and almost rice-like clouds in the lofty sky.

Frost seems also to play a part in sharpening the characteristic odours of winter, such as the smell of cherry-wood or the currant bushes freshly cut by the pruner, of tar when they are dipping hop-poles, the soil newly turned and the roots exposed by the gardeners. And there is a peculiar languid sweetness in the smell of grass when the rime is melting rapidly under the sun. Above all, the fragrance of the weed-fire is never so sweet as when its bluish and white smoke heaves and trails heavily and takes wing at dawn over the frost and its crimson reflections of the flames and among the yellow tassels of the dark hedge.

Country Life, 13th February 1909

February in Wales

From London, I remember, we travelled to the county of ——, in South Wales. February was making the best of his short life, and leaving March a great deal to undo. 'Is there no religion for the temperate and frigid zones?' asks Thoreau, at the end of his 'Winter Walk'. Round the great open Welsh hearths we found a sufficient creed in the sweet paganisms of a fire worship which in that country insists on a blaze in June; preferring it, since for mental and sentimental warmth the sun is some few millions of miles too distant. Spending such an evening by the fireside, it was pleasant to note a culinary genius which experiments evoked. I know nothing that makes the conversation go more 'trippingly on the tongue' than the discussion of such dainties as hands modestly declared inexperienced will compose out of scant elements.

> *'Matter! with six eggs and a strike of rye meal*
> *I had kept the town till Doomsday, perhaps longer;'*

and with less than old Furnace, the cook in Massinger's play, we did succeed in keeping melancholy from the door. Through the window we saw a grey beggar feeding a party of sparrows with his crumbs—a fine economy, charity reduced to its lowest terms. Not, however, that it was a hard season. But the willows were in bud, and for that very reason—there were so many tender things to look cold—the sting was more keen. All day were seen rapid clouds tumbling past a white

horizon, firmly stamped with the outlines of trees; the willow undulating all together, like a living wave of foliage and limber boughs;
the river flowing out of silver into blue shadow, and again into silver
where the sky bent as if to touch it; leaf and flower of celandine gleaming under the briers; whilst the air was vibrant though windless—
stirred like water in a full vessel when more is still poured in. It was the
most perfect of days. The air had all the sparkling purity of winter. It
had, too, something of the mettle and gusto of the spring. The scent of
young grass, uncontested by any flower or fruit, was sharp though
faint, and thus the air was touched with a summer perfume. Now and
then a blackbird fluted a stave or two. But the silence was mysteriously
great, because the incalculably subtle sound of the ocean was over
there, solemnizing, deepening, and as it were charging with 'large
utterance' the silence it could not break. The whole countryside of
grassy level and rolling copse was like a shell put to the ear. For the
shore was never still. A little way out the fisher boats might be curtsey-
ing on the tranquil tide; but reaching the shore, the same tide came
upon fantastic rocks that were an organ out of which it contrived an
awful music. Under the beams of the rocking moon, those tall, cada-
verous crags rose up like stripped reapers, gigantic and morose, reaping and amassing the dolorous harvest of wrecks, waist-deep in a surge
whose waves seemed not to flow and change, but to turn, turn cease-
lessly in the contracted corridors among the rocks, like wheels revolving, and bespattered by the foam that huddled, yellow, coagulate,
quaking, in the crevices.

Soon afterward snow fell, apparently making the air meeter for its
freight of scent from the first violets, which certainly smelt sweeter
than they had ever done before. The strong bells were choked by snow,
and tinkled very timidly in the church. Lightly clothed by the same
fall, the pillared tower of white stone looked wonderfully radiant in the
moonlight, as if fresh from the footsteps of angels or garnished for a
day of extraordinary celebration. Then, too, was the bell note sweetest,
though always unequalled in pure aerial quality, because

'We cannot see, but feel that it is there,'

hid as it is in some dim belfry or mossy turret from which one never
expects so fine a voice.

As we passed upward to the hills, one day, the snow was fading in the sun, and the laurels rose suddenly up as they shook it off in shower after shower. On one hand the ghost of a distant mountain hung lighter than cloud. For a moment another snow shower fell, but settled only on the scattered green of the arable fields: so on that hand lay miles of dark land under a veil of delicatest cirrus. Two miles ahead, on the boldest height of all, was the ruin—the mere dust and ashes—of a castle, pale, continually lost among clouds of which it seemed a part, and as unreal as if it were still in 'the region of stories', and we were reading of it in the monkish chronicle.

The path followed one side of a steep wooded valley, and at the bottom a mountain river ran fast over great stones, its noise muffled by the trees, as if it talked in its beard. For almost a mile we could hear the sounding smoke of a white cataract which gave the river its speed. The great marsh marigolds had come. Fragments of an ancient wall stood here and there among the trees: the stones were blessed with mosses, in whose miniature forests an autumnal red prevailed, which, however, loaded with dew, turned to perfect silver in the sun.

Rose Acre Papers

March Doubts

All day the winter seemed to have gone. The horses' hoofs on the moist, firm road made a clear 'cuck-oo' as they rose and fell; and far off, for the first time in the year, a ploughboy, who remembered spring and knew that it would come again, shouted 'Cuckoo! cuckoo!'

A warm wind swept over the humid pastures and red sand-pits on the hills and they gleamed in a lightly muffled sun. Once more in the valleys the ruddy farmhouses and farm-buildings seemed new and fair again, and the oast-house cones stood up as prophets of spring, since the south wind had turned all their white vanes towards the north, and they felt the sea that lay—an easy journey on such a day—beyond the third or fourth wooded ridge in the south. The leaves of goose-grass, mustard, vetch, dog's mercury, were high above the dead leaves on hedge banks. Primrose and periwinkle were blossoming. Like flowers were the low ash-tree boles where the axe had but lately cut off the tall rods; flower-like and sweet also the scent from the pits where labourers dipped the freshly peeled ash poles in tar. In the elms, sitting crosswise on a bough, sang thrush and missel-thrush; in the young corn, the larks; the robins in the thorns; and in all the meadows the guttural notes of the rooks were mellowed by love and the sun.

Making deep brown ruts across the empty green fields came the long wagons piled high with faggots; the wheels rumbled; the harness jingled and shone; the horses panted and the carters cracked their whips.

Soon would the first chiff-chaff sing in the young larches; at evening the calm, white, majestic young clouds should lie along the horizon in a clear and holy air: and climbing a steep hill at that hour, the walker should see a window, as it were, thrown open in the sky and hear a music that should silence thought and even regret—as when, on the stage, a window is opened and someone invisible is heard to sing a heavy-laden song below it.

But as I walked and the wind fell for the sunset, the path led me under high, stony beeches. The air was cool and still and moist and waterish dark, and no bird sang. A wood-pigeon spread out his barry tail as he ascended perpendicularly to a hidden place among the branches, and then there was no sound. The waterish half-light seemed to have lasted for ever and to have an eternity ahead. Through the trees a grassy, deeply-rutted road wound downwards, and at the edge the ruts were broad and full of dark water. Still retaining some corruption of the light of the sky upon its surface, that shadowed water gave an immense melancholy to the wood. The reflections of the beeches across it were as the bars of a cage that imprisoned some child of light. It was but a few inches deep of rain, and yet, had it been a legendary pool, or had a drowned woman's hair been stamped into the mud at its edge and left a green forehead exposed, it could not have stained and filled the air more tragically. The cold, the silence, the leaflessness found an expression in that clouded shining surface among the ruts. Life and death seemed to contend there, and I recalled a dream which I had lately dreamed.

I dreamed that someone had cut the cables that anchored me to such tranquillity as had been mine, and that I was drifted out upon an immensity of desolation and solitude. I was without hope, without even the energy of despair that might in time have given birth to hope. But in that desolation I found one business: to search for a poison that should kill slowly, painlessly, and unexpectedly. In that search I lost sight of what had persuaded me to it; yet when at last I succeeded, I took a draught and went out into the road and began to walk. A calm fell upon me such as I had sometimes found in June thunderstorms on lonely hills, or in midnights when I stepped for a moment after long foolish labours to my door, and heard the nightingales singing out from the Pleiades that overhung the wood, and saw the flower-faced owl sitting on the gate. I walked on, not hastening with a too great desire nor lingering with a too careful quietude. It was as yet early morning, and the wheat sheaves stood on the gentle hills like yellow-haired women kneeling to the sun that was about to rise. Now and then I passed the corners of villages, and sometimes at windows and through doorways I saw the faces of men and women I had known and seemed to forget, and they smiled and were glad, but not more glad than I. Labouring in the fields also were men whose faces I was happy to recognize and see smiling with recognition. And very sweet it was to go on thus, at ease, knowing neither trouble nor fatigue. I could have gone on, it seemed, for ever, and I wished to live so for ever, when suddenly I remembered the poison. Then of each one I met I begged a remedy. Some reminded me that formerly I had made a poor thing of life, and said that it was too late. Others supposed that I jested. A few asked me to stay with them and rest. The sky and the earth, and the men and women drank of the poison that I had drunken, so that I could not endure the use of my eyes, and I entered a shop to buy some desperate remedy that should end all at once, when, seeing behind the counter a long-dead friend in wedding attire, I awoke.

Even so in the long wet ruts did the false hope of spring contend with the shadows: even so at last did it end, when the dead leaves upon the trees began to stir madly in the night wind, with the sudden, ghastly motion of burnt paper on a still fire when a draught stirs it in a silent room at night; and even the nearest trees seemed to be but fantastic hollows in the misty air.

The Heart of England

But These Things Also

But these things also are Spring's—
On banks by the roadside the grass
Long-dead that is greyer now
Than all the Winter it was;

The shell of a little snail bleached
In the grass; chip of flint, and mite
Of chalk; and the small birds' dung
In splashes of purest white:

All the white things a man mistakes
For earliest violets
Who seeks through Winter's ruins
Something to pay Winter's debts,

While the North blows, and starling flocks
By chattering on and on
Keep their spirits up in the mist,
And Spring's here, Winter's not gone.

Collected Poems

The First Cuckoo

In each spring, as in each man's youth, all things are new, and the finer
our feelings the more numerous and powerful the impressions made on
them. As life or the year advances new things appear continually, the
old are repeated or varied, both by chance and design; multitudinous-
ness, coupled often with decrease of sensibility, reduces the impres-

sions, in number, in power, or in both. Countless are the things which
may impress us for ever. It may be the sound of bells pealing, it may be
the smell of glue on a toy dissolving in a hot bath. But the majority fade
away or can be revived only by poetry or strange chance. Very few
endure. Those that do, most men are pleased and even proud to recall
over and over again.

Usually it is supposed that the first experience makes the lasting impression, and by a kind of natural superstition a special importance is
attached to 'first' experiences, even when of a kind that can be repeated.
Instinctively, but not unconsciously, we prepare ourselves in a reverent
or enthusiastic manner for the first sight of a house or tree or hill
which has a meaning for ourselves only. And so with unexpected re-
curring things of universal significance, like the appearance of the new
moon, or of the faint Pleiades in early autumn. Almost everyone is
pleased to report the crescent moon low in the west on a fine evening:
many probably have an exaltation, however faint or indeterminate, at
the sight, which they have no idea what to do with. Thus many times
a year we enjoy in a milder, more Epicurean way, something like an
imitation of a real first experience. I am not forgetting how much of
the thrill may be due to the feeling of a fresh start, combined with that
of being an old inhabitant of the earth.

But the first cry of the cuckoo in spring is more to us than the new
moon. The first flicker and twitter of the swallow is its only possible
rival. The first snowdrop, the first blackbird's song or peewit's love
cry, the first hawthorn leaves, are as nothing even to those who regard
them, compared with the cuckoo's note, while there are many for
whom it is the one powerfully significant natural thing throughout the
year, apart from broad gradual changes, such as the greening or the
baring of the woods. The old become fearful lest they should not hear
it: having heard it, they fear lest it should be for the last time. It has
been accepted as the object upon which we concentrate whatever feeling we have towards the beginning of spring. It constitutes a natural,
unmistakable festival. We wish to hear it, we are eager and anxious
about it, we pause when it reaches us, as if perhaps it might be bringing
more than it ever brought yet. Vaguely enough, as a rule, we set much
store by this first hearing, and the expectancy does not fail to bring its
reward of at least a full and intense impression. And for this purpose
the cuckoo's note is perfectly suited. It is loud, clear, brief, and distinct,
never in danger of being lost in a chorus of its own or another kind: it

has a human and also a ghostly quality which earns it the reputation of sadness or joyousness at different times.

When we hear a bird's note for the first time in spring, it usually happens that conditions are favourable. If rain is falling or wind roaring in tossing branches, any noise but a loud or near one may be drowned; also mere cold and cloudiness, if they do not keep us indoors, suffice to put us out of the humour for expecting. Thus only naturalists are likely, as a rule, to hear the 'first' note in conditions which are unfavourable, that is to say, which will not further its effect. Again, if we have minds bent on other things or altogether troubled and self-centred, the chances are against hearing it. Company and conversation, the sounds of men or horses or wheels, have the same effect as rain or wind. Thus we often first hear the cuckoo in the first mild, quiet weather of spring, with minds more or less tranquil. If I hear it so, though I cannot imagine anyone less superstitious, I have a feeling of luck. Nine or ten years ago, I remember hearing the cuckoo sing for the first time when I had started out for the day. The bird was slanting down towards our plum-trees and cuckooing there, so that I could not help running home in the hope that I should be first to tell the news.

When I heard it this April, I could not be wholly absorbed in it, yet something of me was carried away, floating in a kind of bliss over the river between the hills. I had been walking all day in Carmarthenshire in hot, bright weather. But no mossy lane overhung by ash trees, no little valley of ivy-mantled oaks or gorse blossoming, no crooked orchard above the roadside, no bushy, dripping precipices that echoed to the gulls' cry on pale sand and white serpentine water, possessed a cuckoo. One bird I heard for the first time that morning—a corncrake in a thicket of thorn and sallow by Goose's Bridge. But at the moment I had no wish to hear that wooden comb scraped. It is a sound for the mowing grass, for the height and heat of midsummer. I was, in fact, irritated by hearing this undesired, unseasonable call already, before the cuckoo's note which I had been listening for during a whole, fine week. Then some hours later I was returning by that same road between Laugharne and St. Clear's. I did not pass one man, woman, or child, for each of the four practically houseless miles. It is a road that rises and falls in following the direction of the Taf, and keeps usually in sight below it the loops of the river, the rushy levels and the low hills opposite, divided by dark hedges with a few red ploughlands and many green pastures, with a scattering of gorse. The corresponding hills

crossed or skirted by my road on this side, were similar. The mile between the hills was silent. It being then after seven and the sun having
just fallen crimson upon my right, the air was still and cool, the sky
cloudless as it had been all day.

The road was deep in dust, but the marigolds in the ditch preserved
their brightness and their coolness. Coming over the shoulder of the
hill called Pwll y Pridd, by the farm Morfa Bach, where the primroses
were so thick under the young emerald larches, I began to have a
strong desire—almost amounting to a conviction—that I should hear
the cuckoo. When I was down again at Goose's Bridge, by the brook
that descends out of a furzy valley towards the Taf, I heard it, or
thought I did. I stopped. Not a sound. I went on stealthily that I might
stop as soon as I heard anything. Again I seemed to hear it; again it had
gone by the time I was still. The third time I had no doubt. The cuckoo
was singing over on the far side of the valley, perhaps three-quarters of
a mile away, probably in a gorse bank just above the marsh. For half a
minute he sang, changed his perch unseen and sang again, his notes as
free from the dust and heat as the cups of the marigolds, and as soft as
the pale white-blue sky, and as dim as the valley into whose twilight
he was gathered, calling fainter and fainter, as I drew towards home.

The Last Sheaf

Spring—Hampshire

Next day the wind has flown and the snow is again almost rain: there
is ever a hint of pale sky above, but it is not as luminous as the earth.
The trees over the road have a beauty of darkness and moistness.
Beyond them the earth is a sainted corpse, with a blue light over it that
is fast annihilating all matter and turning the landscape to a spirit only.
Night and the snow descend upon it, and at dawn the nests are full of
snow. The yews and junipers on a league of Downs are chequered
white upon white slopes, and the green larches support cirrus clouds of
snow. In the garden the daffodils bend criss-cross under snow that cannot quite conceal the yellow flowers. But the snow has ceased. The sky
is at first pale without a cloud and tender as from a long imprisonment;
it deepens in hue as the sun climbs and gathers force. The crooked

paths up the Downs begin to glitter like streaks of lightning. The
thrushes sing. From the straight dark beeches the snow cannot fall fast
enough in great drops, in showers, in masses that release the boughs
with a quiver and a gleam. The green leaves close to the ground creep
out, and against them the snow is blue. A little sighing wind rustles ivy
and juniper and yew. The sun mounts, and from his highest battlement
of cloud blows a long blast of light over the pure land. Once more the
larch is wholly green, the beech rosy brown with buds. A cart goes
by all a-gleam with a load of crimson-sprouting swedes and yellow-
sprouting mangolds that seem to be burning through the net of snow
above them. Down each side of every white road runs a stream that
sings and glitters in ripples like innumerable crystal flowers. Water
drips and trickles and leaps and gushes and oozes everywhere, and
extracts the fragrance of earth and green and flowers under the heat
that hastens to undo the work of the snow. The air is hot and wet. The
snow is impatient to be water again. It still makes a cape over the briers
and brambles, and there is a constant drip and steam and song of drops
from the crossing branches in the cave below. Loud sounds the voice of
leaf and branch and imprisoned water in the languor and joy of their
escape. On every hand there is a drip of gush and ooze of water, a
crackle and rustle and moan of plants and trees unfolding and unbend-
ing and greeting air and light; a close, humid, many-perfumed host;
wet gloom and a multitudinous glitter; a movement of water and of
the shadows like puffs of smoke that fleet over the white fields under
the clouds.

    And over and through it a cuckoo is crying, first overhead, and then
afar, and gradually near and retreating again. He is soon gone, but the
ears are long afterwards able to extract the spirit of the song, the
exact interval of it, from among all the lasting sounds, until we hear it
as clearly as before, out of the blue sky, out of the white cloud, out of
the shining grey water. It is a word of power—cuckoo! The melting of
the snow is faster than ever, and at the end of the day there is none left
except in some hollows of the Downs on the slopes behind the topmost
of the beeches that darkly fringe the violet sky. In the misty shutting of
the light there are a thousand songs laced by cuckoos' cries and the first
hooting of owls, and the beeches have become merely straight lines of
pearl in a mist of their own boughs. Below them, in the high woods,
goes on the fall of the melting snow through the gloomy air, and the
splash on the dead leaves. This gloom and monotonous sound make an

exquisite cloister, visited but not disturbed by the sound of the blackbirds singing in the mist of the vale underneath. Slowly the mist has
deepened from the woods to the vale and now the eye cannot see from
tree to tree. Then the straight heavy rain descends upon the songs and
the clatterings of blackbirds, and when they are silenced the moorhen's
watery hoot announces that the world belongs to the beasts and the
rainy dark until tomorrow.

The South Country

Bright Clouds

Bright clouds of may
Shade half the pond.
Beyond,
All but one bay
Of emerald
Tall reeds
Like criss-cross bayonets
Where a bird once called,
Lies bright as the sun.
No one heeds.
The light wind frets
And drifts the scum
Of may-blossom.
Till the moorhen calls
Again
Naught's to be done
By birds or men.
Still the may falls.

Collected Poems

May Song

Fine sounds are floating wild
About the earth.

KEATS

A crowded woodland of varied hues, ledge beyond ledge, climbs the hill's slow ascent, and in this dazzling dawn the sunlight plays upon the dewed leaves with gorgeous effect. Mellow limes contrast with sea-green chestnuts, now flaming with pinnacles of waxen bloom; the reddened foliage of the oaks seems to burn in the fierce light, while the pale tasselled birches are all a-quiver; and at the margin frail poplars change from grey to silver—whitening, as their leaves turn, with undersides uppermost, in the wind. The parched ploughland sloping to the wood glows rust-red, though shadowed at its borders by tall thorns just crowned with the silver-white of May blossom. Yonder, where the ridge dips to the north among dark meadow-tracts, the gleaming roofs and glittering spires of a silent town pierce the pale sky. Coils of wood-smoke from the keeper's cottage, with grey thatched roof and russet chimney-stack, drift lightly in the clear atmosphere, draping a corner of the wood as with a blue translucent haze. Flaring lights of gold and purple fade in the eye of day, and barred clouds drive slowly over from the west.

The rarely trodden meadow-path and the taller grass around is hoary with dew; but as it enters the hazel gloom the scattered blades do but faintly twinkle in their sheathing crystal. Tender hyacinths that open bell by bell each morning are washed with a finer hue which must vanish with scorching-noon; and the little spring-vetch, mounting with spray over spray of narrow leaflets to the lowest hazel-boughs, is for the moment gay with its solitary purple flower. Tiny caterpillars, on which the whitethroat preys, seem to hang from the oaks by silver gossamers, and their own bodies are clear as amber in the delicate half-light, half-gloom, that dwells as yet in the wood's shadow. Through this weird light the early willow wrens chase one another with twirling motions like butterfles; then in the nut bushes or the broad oaks they sing their tender threnody, playing among the slender swaying twigs. In the deeper shadows, far among the oaks, jays squeal and chatter, drowning half the music of the wood. Suddenly, with a flash of blue-pied pinions, a jay leaves a tree where a nest of oak twigs and woven rootlets, yellow and stiff as cocoanut fibre, is hidden amid thorny boughs—a hoarse cry and a flutter of wings through the leaves following her flight. Blackbird and thrush steal across the lawn-like walks between roofing arcades of oak, halting half way over to pull a worm or to listen for a while. Unsheltered and in full view the blackbird displays a grotesque mixture of daring and timidity—in his hurried though bold-seeming progress, with ducking head, and in the chiding yet half-exultant chuckle with which he slips away into cover. In his mellow music alone there lurks no sign of doubt or fear.

The Woodland Life

June

June puts bronze and crimson on many of her leaves. The maple-leaves and many of the leaves of thorn and bramble and dogwood are rosy; the hazel-leaves are rosy-brown; the herb-robert and parsley are rose-red; the leaves of ash and holly are dark lacquered. The copper beeches, opulently sombre under a faintly yellowed sky, seem to be the sacred trees of the thunder that broods above. Presently the colour of the threat is changed to blue, which soiled white clouds pervade until the whole sky is woolly white and grey and moving north. There is no wind, but there is a roar as of a hurricane in the trees far off; soon it is louder, in the trees not so remote; and in a minute the rain has traversed half a mile of woods, and the distant combined roar is swallowed up by the nearer pattering on roof and pane and leaf, the dance of leaves, the sway of branches, the trembling of whole trees under the flood. The rain falls straight upon the hard road, and each drop seems to leap upward from it barbed. Great drops dive among the motionless, dusty nettles. The thunder unloads its ponderous burden upon the resonant floor of the sky; but the sounds of the myriad leaves and grass-blades drinking all but drowns the boom, the splitting roar, and the echo in the hills. When it is over it has put a final sweetness into the

blackbird's voice and into the calm of the evening garden when the
voice of a singer does but lay another tribute at the feet of the enormous
silence. Frail is that voice as the ghost-moth dancing above the grass so
faithfully that it seems a flower attached to a swaying stem, or as the
one nettle-leaf that flutters in a draught of the hedge like a signalling
hand while all the rest of the leaves are as if they could not move
again, or as the full moon that is foundering on a white surf in the
infinite violet sky. More large and more calm and emptier of familiar
things grows the land as I pass through it, under the hoverings of the
low-flying but swiftly-turning nightjar, until at midnight only a low
white mist moves over the gentle desolation and warm silence. The
mist wavers, and discloses a sky all strewn with white stars like the
flowers of an immense jessamine. It closes up again, and day is born
unawares in its pale arms, and earth is for the moment nothing but the
tide of downs flowing west and the branch of red roses that hangs
heavily laden and drowsed with its weight and beauty over my path,
dipping its last spray in the dew of the grass.

The day is a Sunday, and no one is on foot or on wheel in the
broad arable country that ripples in squares of green, or brown, or
yellow, or grey, to the green Downs and their dark, high-perched
woods. As if for some invisible beholder, the green elders and their
yellow-green flower-buds make their harmony with the yellow-
lichened barns against which they lean; the grass and the noble trees,
the groups of wayside aspen, the line of horsechestnuts, the wych-elms
on both sides of the road, the one delicate sycamore before the inn and
the company of sycamores above the cross—the spacious thatch and
tiles of the farmyard quadrangle—the day newly painted in white and
blue—the green so green in the hedges, and the white and purple so
pure in the flowers—all seem to be meant for eyes that know nothing
of Time and of what 'brought death into the world and all our woe'.
And in this solitude the young birds are very happy. They have taken
possession of the thick hedges, of the roadside grass, of the roads themselves. They flutter and run and stumble there; they splash in the pools
and in the dust, which not a wheel nor a foot has marked. These at
least are admitted into the kingdom along with that strange wildfowl
that lives 'to maintain the trade and mystery of typographers'.

The South Country

Haymaking

After night's thunder far away had rolled
The fiery day had a kernel sweet of cold,
And in the perfect blue the clouds uncurled,
Like the first gods before they made the world
And misery, swimming the stormless sea
In beauty and in divine gaiety.
The smooth white empty road was lightly strewn
With leaves—the holly's Autumn falls in June—
And fir cones standing up stiff in the heat.
The mill-foot water tumbled white and lit
With tossing crystals, happier than any crowd
Of children pouring out of school aloud.
And in the little thickets where a sleeper
For ever might lie lost, the nettle creeper
And garden-warbler sang unceasingly;
While over them shrill shrieked in his fierce glee
The swift with wings and tail as sharp and narrow
As if the bow had flown off with the arrow.
Only the scent of woodbine and hay new mown
Travelled the road. In the field sloping down,
Park-like, to where its willows showed the brook,
Haymakers rested. The tosser lay forsook
Out in the sun; and the long waggon stood
Without its team: it seemed it never would
Move from the shadow of that single yew.
The team, as still, until their task was due,
Beside the labourers enjoyed the shade
That three squat oaks mid-field together made
Upon a circle of grass and weed uncut,
And on the hollow, once a chalk pit, but
Now brimmed with nut and elder-flower so clean.
The men leaned on their rakes, about to begin,

But still. And all were silent. All was old,
This morning time, with a great age untold,
Older than Clare and Cobbett, Morland and Crome,
Than, at the field's far edge, the farmer's home,
A white house crouched at the foot of a great tree.
Under the heavens that know not what years be
The men, the beasts, the trees, the implements
Uttered even what they will in times far hence—
All of us gone out of the reach of change—
Immortal in a picture of an old grange.

Collected Poems

Summer

The last hay-waggon has hardly rolled between the elms before the reaper and the reaping-machines begin to work. The oats and wheat are in tents over all the land. Then, then it is hard not to walk over the brown in the green of August grass. There is a roving spirit everywhere. The very tents of the corn suggest a bivouac. The white clouds coming up out of the yellow corn and journeying over the blue have set their faces to some goal. The traveller's joy is tangled over the hazels and over the faces of the small chalk-pits. The white beam and the poplar and the sycamore fluttering show the silver sides of their leaves and rustle farewells. The perfect road that goes without hedges under elms and through the corn says, 'Leave all and follow.' How the bridges overleap the streams at one leap, or at three, in arches like those of running hounds! The far-scattered, placid sunsets pave the feet of the spirit with many a road to joy; the huge, vacant halls of dawn give a sense of godlike power.

But it is hard to make anything like a truce between these two incompatible desires, the one for going on and on over the earth, the other that would settle for ever, in one place as in a grave and have nothing to do with change. Suppose a man to receive notice of death, it would be hard to decide whether to walk or sail until the end, seeing no man, or none but strangers; or to sit—alone—and by thinking or not thinking to make the change to come as little as is permitted. The two desires will often painfully alternate. Even on these harvest days there is a temptation to take root for ever in some corner of a field or on some hill from which the world and the clouds can be seen at a distance. For the wheat is as red as the most red sand, and up above it tower the elms, dark prophets persuading to silence and a stillness like their own. Away on the lesser Downs the fields of pale oats are liquid within their border of dark woods; they also propose deep draughts of oblivion and rest. Then, again, there is the field—the many fields— where a regiment of shocks of oats are ranked under the white moon between rows of elms on the level Sussex land not far from the sea. The contrast of the airy matter underfoot and the thin moon over head, with the massy dark trees, as it were suspended between; the numbers and the order of the sheaves; their inviolability, though pro- tected but by the gateway through which they are seen—all satisfy the soul as they can never satisfy the frame. Then there are the mists before heat which make us think of autumn or not, according to our tempers. All night the aspens have been shivering and the owls exulting under a clear full moon and above the silver of a great dew. You climb the steep chalk slope, through the privet and dog-wood coppice; among the scattered junipers—in this thick haze as in darkness they group themselves so as to make fantastic likenesses of mounted men, animals, monsters; over the dead earth in the shade of the broad yews, and thence suddenly under lightsome sprays of guelder-rose and their cherry-coloured berries; over the tufted turf; and then through the massed beeches, cold and dark as a church and silent; and so out to the level waste cornland at the top, to the flints and the clay. There a myriad oriflammes of ragwort are borne up on tall stems of equal height, straight and motionless, and near at hand quite clear, but farther away forming a green mist until, farther yet, all but the flowery surface is invisible, and that is but a glow. The stillness of the green and golden multitudes under the grey mist, perfectly still though a wind flutters the high tops of the beech, has an immortal beauty, and that they should ever change does not enter the mind which is thus for the moment lured happily into a strange confidence and ease. But the sun gains power in the south-east. It changes the mist into a fleeting garment, not of cold or of warm grey, but of diaphanous gold. There is a sea-like moan of wind in the half-visible trees, a wavering of the mist to and fro until it is dispersed far and wide as part of the very light, of the blue shade, of the colour of cloud and wood and down. As the mist is unwoven the ghostly moon is disclosed, and a bank of dead white clouds where the Downs should be. Under the very eye of the veiled sun a golden light and warmth begins to nestle among the mounds of foliage at the surface of the low woods. The beeches close by have got a new voice in their crisp, cool leaves, of which every one is doing something—cool, though the air itself is warm. Woodpigeons coo. The white cloud-bank gives way to an immeasurable half-moon of Downs, some bare, some saddle-backed with woods, and far away and below, out of the ocean of countless trees in the southern veil, a spire. It is a spire which at this hour is doubtless moving a thousand men with a thousand thoughts and hopes and memories of men and causes, but moves me with the thought alone that just a hundred years ago was buried underneath it a child, a little child whose mother's mother was at the pains to inscribe a tablet saying to all who pass by that he was once 'an amiable and most endearing child'.

And what nights there are on the hills. The ashsprays break up the low full moon into a flower of many sparks. The Downs are heaved up into the lighted sky—surely they heave in their tranquillity as with a slowly taken breath. The moon is half-way up the sky and exactly over the centre of the long curve of Downs; just above them lies a long terrace of white cloud, and at their feet gleams a broad pond, the rest of the valley being utterly dark and undistinguishable, save a few scattered lamps and one near meadow that catches the moonlight so as to be transmuted to a lake. But every rainy leaf upon the hill is brighter than any of the few stars above, and from many leaves and blades hang drops as large and bright as the glowworms in their recesses. Larger by a little, but not brighter, are the threes and fours of lights at windows in the valley. The wind has fallen, but a mile of woods un-lading the rain from their leaves make a sound of wind, while each separate drop can be heard from the nearest branches, a noise of rapt content, as if they were telling over again the kisses of the shower. The air itself is heavy as mead with the scent of yew and juniper and thyme.

The South Country

Midsummer

The gold lilies have unclosed on Haweswater, and the wind does not raise the green discs of leaf: the sedge-warblers chatter and sing all day on the sedges above the silver shallows. It is midsummer.

Next to being with spring when it comes to the moors and mountains is being with midsummer. When spring comes it is often, as it were, a lamb snatched from the teeth of winter. It is pale and trembling, a shade overhangs it; it is doubtful, mysterious, and one has need of faith to believe that it will grow up and become strong and bold. But now, with midsummer, it is impossible to suppose that winter can overcome it. And especially in this year of years. There have been no springs like it. The others have led up to this, which must break away from all precedents.

Day after day the wind blows from the south, usually a rainy quarter here, yet no rain falls. Thunder skirts us, an impotent barbaric decoration, a lion that roars like a dove in the gossamer haze veiling Helvellyn northward. Nothing invades this charmed fortress between sea and mountains. A magic circle protects it. It seems to be midsummer itself, an island in the midst of summer, close to the shore of spring, out of sight of autumn. For if it be reasonable as well as customary to call this solstice midsummer, it is because the year leaps forward rapidly up to this point, and then declines—or used to do in the old years—very slowly from the summit. If examined it might prove as transitory as any of the moments of spring. The thunder that hovers circling round us might burst in tonight. But some of the marks of change are less obvious now than in spring. The greens of the leaves are mature, yet will last some time. The fading of blossoms has by midsummer become familiar, and we notice it less than when primroses are being torn, bluebells drying up, may browning and dropping. The succession of flowers has been so continuous that it promises to have no end. The year has outgrown some of the beautiful refinements and perturbations of spring, like the interchanging and overlapping melancholy and excitement of youth.

I have called this a charmed fortress. But it is no garden elaborately guarded and secluded. No Chinese wall has been built to keep out autumn and winter. On the contrary, childlike boldness has placed it where they could never suspect their victim of being so guileless as to hide. It is on a high, open hill-top among rocks and stunted trees, through which I see hills scarred or wooded a mile or two distant, and mountains that might be clouds on the horizon. There is no garden, simply because the rabbits have not been shot. Wild roses, both white and, with butter-coloured hearts, overtop the stone walls in places; otherwise, the noticeable flower is the coral of the Scots firs among young shoots like silver candles. No, it is not a garden; it is but a ground where the sun can dwell all the long day and bank his heat in grass and short bracken and stones. Flowers there are—rock roses of thin yellow silk, and white lady's bedstraw, and thyme—but the bird's-eye primroses, rose-purple clusters smelling like primroses by the waterside, the violet meadow-cranesbills among the dusty nettle and parsley of the roadside, cannot climb here. Higher up, the rock rose fails, and only herb Robert thrusts up a flower among crumbs of stone. There, even some of the grass has withered to a skeleton, and the mosses that were like moles of gilt olive have parched and darkened. Half the hill limestone, now high boulders, now smoothly corrugated pavements, now flakes vertically rotted, now crumbled scree, now flat plates that ring like crockery or like iron. (Years ago someone collected plates of this stone that rang through a whole scale of music.) Sometimes a juniper has penetrated the stones and spread foliage of palest and blackest green out over them in a bush like an umbrella with no handle. But of the junipers the dead are more numerous than the living.

Often I hear no music but the stones ringing as I walk, unless a peewit cries, or a wheatear, flitting about me, says alternately 'chuck' and 'sweet'. Once or twice in the day, far away over the pallid rock and misted dark bushes, a cuckoo calls; not the cuckoo of the South Country, to whom the poet has been repeating for several weeks the line:

Tune thy two strings and break the third.

but a faultless cuckoo. I have not once seen him. He is as vague as Helvellyn northward, or Ingleborough eastward. His note seems an echo, long treasured, and now delivered up by the rocks of Whitbarrow, that make two arched leaps and then fall perpendicularly to the flat river land. His voice skirts us; being a perishing thing it does not really enter the circle.

But the nightjar is the bird of midsummer. At nightfall he perches on the tip of a Scots fir's topmost silver candle and reels his churr. The hum of insects is to midsummer heat what the kettle's singing is to water beginning to boil. The nightjar's 'purr' represents the water seething, bubbling, and lifting the lid. The wind has gone up into Scotland. The air is still. The nightjar fills the broad night with a noise as of a shadowy brook running over the dry, pale rocks of the hills. While he sings, taking breath at moments, he looks from side to side on his perch, then suddenly ends, and slips off silently. His next perch is distant, and I can hear him only if I listen for him. Again he shifts, this time out of hearing. For a time there is no sound on earth, only an owl that cries like a huntsman among the mountains of the moon, winding his horn.

The Last Sheaf

A Little before Harvest

Summer is perfect now.

The wheat says so, when in the dawn it drips with half an hour's rain and gleams like copper under the fresh, dim sky; it cries aloud the same when it crackles in the midday sun, and the golden sea of it washes murmurously to the feet of the hills.

In the hedges and fields the agrimony wands and mullein staves, the climbing vetch, the cushioned bird's-foot lotus, the myriads of ragwort and sow-thistle, are golden too.

The meadowsweet and honeysuckle flowers and the wild carrot seeds give out sweet scents, but not so strong as not to be drowned, when the wind blows, by a thousand lesser scents from field and wood and farmyard.

Wood-pigeons coo in the high-shaded storeys of the beeches and in the wet willow copses where bushes and herbage have grown so dense that hardly a bird's-nester or a lover would care to penetrate them. In the dark wood alleys, all day long, hang insects whose wings seem to be still in their swiftness, like golden lamps.

The gardens have amber lilies, fuchsia trees, phloxes, poppies, holly-hocks, carnations, snapdragons, rockets, and red flax rising above rose of Sharon and lemon-scented balm and yellow stonecrop, where the tortoise-shell butterflies worship with opening wings.

And on the garden walls the purple plums ooze and heave in the sun with yellow wasps that give a touch of horror to the excellent and abounding life of perfect summer.

These things and many more the eye notes carelessly. We are so rich that we do not count our treasure. We record them as contented worshippers their beads. They are but as dust above the corn when the thresher twists his oaken flail. The mother or master of them all seems to be the line of the chalk hills.

The corn sweeps to these hills, and on the strand which divides them is a hamlet of six thatched cottages and a farmhouse, and new hay-stacks round these, fine and sharp-angled, and old ones carved in steps and supported by props of ash. The cream pans and the churns glitter outside the house. A girl kneels at the brook that flows past and dips a jug among the cresses, trying to catch a trout at the same time. The eye dwells on these for a little while, saying that it could be content there never to wander again, and then rises to the downs, and away it goes, soaring as at the sound of organ or harp. For how proud-thoughted are these long, curving downs, whether they make a highway at noon for round white clouds or at night for the large moon. They uplift and allure and lead far away the eye. The mind follows the eye as the streaming wake follows the ship and is naught without it. Those curves suggest to the mind, confused and languid after long summer days in the lowland, that it also might follow such curves that lead on—surely—to noble thoughts and high discoveries, though without them it will be happy merely in following with joyous undulations to the windy beeches on the farthest height. To see them close by with our last glance before entering an inn is good, or, far off, on a midsummer night when we are to watch the sun rise from the encampment which makes one of them, or to fancy them by the winter fire: but to see them thus, in full summer, when day is separate from day only by brief, perfumed nights of stars, stimulates like a page of saga or history or a perfect rhyme, setting the heart free. 'Let us be brave', says a shepherd of these hills.

In lofty numbers let us rave . . .
I'll borrow Phoebus' fiery jades,
With which about the world he trades,
    And put them in my plough.

I'll to great Jove, hap good, hap ill,
Though he with thunder threat to kill,
    And beg of him a boon.

To swerve up one of Cynthia's beams,
And there to bathe thee in the streams
    Discover'd in the moon. . . .

And to those indraughts I'll thee bring,
That wondrous and eternal Spring,
    Whence the ocean hath its flowing.

We'll down to the dark House of Sleep,
Where snoring Morpheus doth keep,
    And wake the drowsy groom.

And at evening, when the rooks go over, quietly expounding space in the rosy sky, they do not, as in other countries they do, torment the mind; for the ridge of the downs travels the same way and is at the same moment here, just above us, and yonder in the bosom of the sunset, and it gives rest and satisfaction as, but a few hours ago, it gave infinite adventure and happiness therewith.

The Heart of England

The End of Summer

All night—for a week—it rains, and at last there is a still morning of mist. A fire of weeds and hedge-clippings in a little flat field is smouldering. The ashes are crimson, and the bluish-white smoke flows in a divine cloudy garment round the boy who rakes over the ashes. The heat is great, and the boy, straight and well made, wearing close

F

gaiters of leather that reach above the knees, is languid at his task, and often leans upon his rake to watch the smoke coiling away from him like a monster reluctantly fettered, and sometimes bursting into an anger of sprinkled sparks. He adds some wet hay, and the smoke pours out of it like milky fleeces when the shearer reveals the inmost wool with his shears. Above and beyond him the pale blue sky is dimly white-clouded over beech woods whose many greens and yellows and yellow-greens are softly touched by the early light which cannot penetrate to the blue caverns of shade underneath. Athwart the woods rises a fount of cottage-smoke from among mellow and dim roofs. Under the smoke and partly scarfed at times by a drift from it is the yellow of sunflower and dahlia, the white of anemone, the tenderest green and palest purple of a thick cluster of autumn crocuses that have broken out of the dark earth and stand surprised, amidst their own weak light as of the underworld from which they have come. Robins sing among the fallen apples, and the cooing of wood-pigeons is attuned to the soft light and the colours of the bowers. The yellow apples gleam. It is the gleam of melting frost. Under all the dulcet warmth of the face of things lurks the bitter spirit of the cold. Stand still for more than a few moments and the cold creeps with a warning, and then a menace into the breast. That is the bitterness that makes this morning of all others in the year so mournful in its beauty. The colour and the grace invite to still contemplation and long draughts of dream; the frost compels to motion. The scent is that of wood-smoke, of fruit and of some fallen leaves. This is the beginning of the pageant of autumn, of that gradual pompous dying which has no parallel in human life, yet draws us to it with sure bonds. It is a dying of the flesh, and we see it pass through a kind of beauty which we can only call spiritual, of so high and inaccessible a strangeness is it. The sight of such perfection as is many times achieved before the end awakens the never more than lightly sleeping human desire of permanence. Now, now is the hour; let things be thus; thus for ever; there is nothing further to be thought of; let these remain. And yet we have a premonition that re-main they must not for more than a little while. The motion of the autumn is a fall, a surrender, requiring no effort, and therefore the mind cannot long be blind to the cycle of things as in the spring it can when the effort and delight of ascension veils the goal and the decline beyond. A few frosts now, a storm of wind and rain, a few brooding mists, and the woods that lately hung dark and massive and strong upon the steep hills are transfigured and have become cloudily light and full of change and ghostly fair; the crowing of a cock in the still misty morning echoes up in the many-coloured trees like a challenge to the spirits of them to come out and be seen, but in vain. For months the woods have been homely and kind, companions and backgrounds to our actions and thoughts, the wide walls of a mansion utterly our own. We could have gone on living with them for ever. We had given up the ardours, the extreme ecstasy of our first bridal affection, but we had not forgotten them. We could not become indifferent to the Spanish chestnut trees that grow at the top of the steep rocky banks on either side of the road and mingle their foliage overhead. Of all trees well-grown chestnuts are among the most pleasant to look up at. For the foliage is not dense and it is for the most part close to the large boughs, so that the light comes easily down through all the horizontal leaves, and the shape of each separate one is not lost in the multitude, while at the same time the bold twists of the branches are undraped or easily seen through such translucent green. The trunks are crooked, and the handsome deep furrowing of the bark is often spirally cut. The limbs are few and wide apart so as to frame huge delicately lighted and shadowed chambers of silence or of birds' song. The leaves turn all together to a leathern hue, and when they fall stiffen and display their shape on the ground and long refuse to be merged in the dismal trodden hosts. But when the first one floats past the eye and is blown like a canoe over the pond we recover once more our knowledge and fear of Time. All those ladders of goose-grass that scaled the hedges of spring are dead grey; they are still in their places, but they clamber no longer. The chief flower is the yellow bloom set in the dark ivy round the trunks of the ash trees; and where it climbs over the holly and makes a solid sunny wall, and in the hedges, a whole people of wasps and wasp-like flies are always at the bloom with crystal wings, except when a passing shadow disperses them for a moment with one buzz. But these cannot long detain the eye from the crumbling woods in the haze or under the large white clouds—from the amber and orange bracken about our knees and the blue recesses among the distant golden beeches when the sky is blue but beginning to be laden with loose rain-clouds, from the line of leaf-tipped poplars that bend against the twilight sky; and there is no scent of flowers to hide that of dead leaves and rotting fruit. We must watch it until the end, and gain slowly the philosophy or the memory or the forgetfulness that fits us for accepting winter's boon. Pauses there are, of course, or what seem pauses in the declining of this pomp; afternoons when the rooks waver and caw over their beechen town and the pigeons coo content; dawns when the white mist is packed like snow over the vale and the high woods take the level beams and a hundred globes of dew glitter on every thread of the spiders' hammocks or loose perpendicular nets among the thorns, and through the mist rings the anvil a mile away with a music as merry as that of the daws that soar and dive between the beeches and the spun white cloud; mornings full of the sweetness of mushrooms and black-berries from the short turf among the blue scabious bloom and the gorgeous brier; empurpled evenings before frost when the robin sings passionate and shrill and from the garden earth float the smells of a hundred roots with messages of the dark world; and hours full of the thrush's soft November music. The end should come in heavy and lasting rain. At all times I love rain, the early momentous thunderdrops, the perpendicular cataract shining, or at night the little showers, the spongy mists, the tempestuous mountain rain. I like to see it possessing the whole earth at evening, smothering civilization, taking away from me myself everything except the power to walk under the dark trees and to enjoy as humbly as the hissing grass, while some twinkling house-light or song sung by a lonely man gives a foil to the immense dark force. I like to see the rain making the streets, the railway station, a pure desert, whether bright with lamps or not. It foams off the roofs and trees and bubbles into the water-butts. It gives the grey rivers a demonic majesty. It scours the roads, sets the flints moving, and exposes the glossy chalk in the tracks through the woods. It does work that will last as long as the earth. It is about eternal business. In its noise and myriad aspect I feel the mortal beauty of immortal things. And then after many days the rain ceases at midnight with the wind, and in the silence of dawn and frost the last rose of the world is dropping her petals down to the glistering whiteness, and there they rest blood-red on the winter's desolate coast.

The South Country

September

The other night I awoke just as the robin was beginning to sing outside in the dark garden. Beyond him the wind made a moan in the little fir-copse as of a forest in a space magically enclosed and silent, and in the intervals of his song silence fell about him like a cloak which the wind could not penetrate. As well as I knew the triple cry farther off for the crow of the first cock, I knew this for the robin's song, pausing but unbroken, though it was unlike any song of robin I had heard in daylight, standing or walking among trees. Outside, in the dark bush, to me lying prostrate, patient, unmoving, the song was absolutely monotonous, absolutely expressionless, a chain of little thin notes linked mechanically in a rhythm identical at each repetition. This was not the voluntary personal utterance of a winged sprite that I used to know, but a note touched on the instrument of night by a player unknown to me, save that it was he who delighted in the moaning fir-trees and in my silence. Nothing intelligible to me was expressed by it; since he, the player, alone knew, I call it expressionless.

When the light began to arrive, the song in the enclosed hush, and the sound of the trees beyond it, remained the same. I remained awake, silently and as stilly as possible, cringing for sleep. I was an unwilling note on the instrument; yet I do not know that the robin was less unwilling. I strove to escape out of that harmony of bird, wind, and man. But as fast as I make my mind a faintly heaving, shapeless, grey blank, some form or colour appeared; memory or anticipation was at work.

Gradually I found myself trying to understand this dawn harmony. I vowed to remember it and ponder it in the light of day. To make sure of remembering I tried putting it into rhyme. I was resolved not to omit the date; and so much so that the first line had to be 'The seventh of September', nor could I escape from this necessity. Then September was to be rhymed with. The word 'ember' occurred and stayed; no other would respond to my calling. The third and fourth lines, it seemed, were bound to be something like—

F*

The sere and the ember
Of the year and of me.

This gave me no satisfaction, but although I was under a very strong compulsion I could do no more; not a line would add itself to the wretched three; nor did they cease to return again and again to my head. It was fortunate for me as a man, if not as an unborn poet, that I could not forget the lines; for by continual helpless repetition of them I rose yet once more to the weakness that sleep demanded. Gradually I became conscious of nothing but the moan of trees, the monotonous expressionless robin's song, the slightly aching body to which I was, by ties more and more slender, attached. I felt, I knew, I did not think that there would always be an unknown player, always wind and trees, always a robin singing, always a listener listening in the stark dawn: and I knew also that if I were the listener I should not always lie thus in a safe warm bed thinking myself alive. . . . And so I fell asleep again on the seventh of September.

The Last Sheaf

October

The green elm with the one great bough of gold
Lets leaves into the grass slip, one by one,—
The short hill grass, the mushrooms small, milk-white,
Harebell and scabious and tormentil,
That blackberry and gorse, in dew and sun,
Bow down to; and the wind travels too light
To shake the fallen birch leaves from the fern;
The gossamers wander at their own will.
At heavier steps than birds' the squirrels scold.
The rich scene has grown fresh again and new
As Spring and to the touch is not more cool
Than it is warm to the gaze; and now I might
As happy be as earth is beautiful,
Were I some other or with earth could turn
In alternation of violet and rose,

Harebell and snowdrop, at their season due,
And gorse that has no time not to be gay.
But if this be not happiness,—who knows?
Some day I shall think this a happy day,
And this mood by the name of melancholy
Shall no more blackened and obscurèd be.

Collected Poems

In Autumn Woods

So late in autumn we hardly look for the beauty of flowers. One short hedgemound, however, displays quite a number of dainty blossoms. Thick as daisies on a lawn, the tiny field-speedwells stud the exposed side of the slope; their leaves are still a tender green, and the blue of the flowers equals that of the veronica of May, while this we treasure for its lateness. In the brambles above there are still a few pale petals, but sadly torn and discoloured by wind and frost. Another late blossom is the golden cinquefoil, with its pretty five-branched leaves trailing hither and thither. Though long dead, the tall docks yet defy the season, and raise aloft a slender spike of deep red, singularly like the sorrel-tips that toned the buttercup fields of midsummer. Like the docks, the teasels are grey and dry and brittle, but look strong as ever, growing from the shallow ditch, and rearing their tall stalks and prickly plumes almost to the hedge-top. But perhaps the rarest of all these flowers of the fall is one little spray of hawthorn bloom. Though so inseparably connected with spring, it is here in the drooping of the year, with its snowy petals and delicious fragrance. This single group of florets recalls the May day, just after the swifts came, when first the dewy green of the hawthorn was dappled with flakes of blossom, and the call of the cuckoo was heard in the land. How changed the scene since then!

Five teams are engaged in ploughing up a broad sloping meadow, where the blood-red clover grew, and about the steaming horses the rooks are wheeling and settling here and there. Over the same field flocks of larks and finches are flitting, seldom staying long in the damp furrows among the brown clods that hide them so completely. A moment ago two larks were straining in song high above their fellows and the quarrelsome rooks; and, what is rare in autumn, their notes were uttered with the old persistence and charm. Along the blackthorn hedge blackbirds start out now and again with their peculiar nervous chuckle, so irritating to the sportsman, but a note of warning to other birds. They hesitate to leave the cover of the hedge, for it is a long flight to the gorse opposite, and eventually determine to rely on the shelter of the dead grasses that thickly envelop the blackthorn-stems. Before we have long passed them, their hilarity, so long subdued, bursts out in a defiant shriek as they follow one another up into the pollard oaks.

In the dense green coverts of the summer hedgerows nests were difficult to find, but now they show at every turn. The cunning basket-work of the lesser whitethroat, so frail as to seem incapable of holding the smallest egg, is filled with rotting black leaves and haws that have dropped thus early. Screened by the trailing dog-rose branches are heads of yarrow-flower and a few worn dandelions, mingling with the purple that stains the woodbine drooping almost to earth, and with the crimson of the blackberry foliage. With the failing light that precedes sundown, a blackbird and a thrush join their notes and delight for a while the ear, now all unused to such harmonies of woodland song.

The Woodland Life

Digging
ᴇᴤᵻᴥᴧ

Today I think
Only with scents,—scents dead leaves yield,
And bracken, and wild carrot's seed,
And the square mustard field;

Odours that rise
When the spade wounds the root of tree,
Rose, currant, raspberry, or goutweed,
Rhubarb or celery;

The smoke's smell, too,
Flowing from where a bonfire burns

The dead, the waste, the dangerous,
And all to sweetness turns.

It is enough
To smell, to crumble the dark earth,
While the robin sings over again
Sad songs of Autumn mirth.

Collected Poems

November

The night had almost come, and the rain had not ceased, among the hills of an unknown country. Behind me, twelve desolate miles of hill and sky away, was a village; and on the way to it, half-a-dozen farms; and before me were three or four houses scattered over two or three miles of winding lanes, with an inn and a church. The parson had just come away from his poultry, and as his wife crossed the road with her apron over her head, I asked where the inn was, and whether it had a room ready in the winter. Two minutes after she had seen me—if she could see me in the dark lane—she had told me that if the inn had no room, I was not to go farther, but to stay at the vicarage. But the inn had a bed to spare, and there was good beer to be had by a great fire in a room shining with brass and pewter, and overhead guns and hams and hanks of wool; and the hostess was jocund, stout, and young, and not only talkative but anxious to be talked to, and she had that maternal kindness—or shall I call it the kindness of a very desirable aunt?— towards strangers, which I have always found in Welsh women, young and old, in the villages and on the moors. So there I stayed and listened to the rain and the fire and the landlady's rich, humming voice uttering and playing strange tricks with English. I was given a change of clothing as if I had asked and paid for it. Then I went to the vicarage, and because I said I loved Welsh hymns and Welsh voices the vicar and his wife and daughter, without unction or preparation or a piano, sang to me, taking parts, some tremendous hymns and some gay melodies,

Whence banished is the roughness of our years,

which made the rain outside seem April rain. They sang, and told me about the road I was to follow, until I had to go to my inn.

Next day, after paying what I liked at the inn, and promising the hostess that I would learn Welsh, I walked for twenty miles over stony roads gleaming with rain upon the white thorns and bloom on the sloes, and through woods where nothing brooded solemnly over grey moss and green moss on the untrodden, rotten wood, and up dry, ladder-like beds of brooks that served as paths, over peat and brindled grass, and along golden hazel hedges, where grew the last meadow-sweet with herb-robert and harebell and one wild rose, and above little valleys of lichened ash trees; and sometimes beneath me, and sometimes high above, the yellow birches waved in the rain, like sunset clouds fettered to the ground and striving and caracoling in their fetters.

Again I came at nightfall to a strange farmhouse, and was honoured by being asked into the kitchen; again I was given dry clothes. The juicy mutton broke up like game. The farmer sang to me from the Welsh hymn-book and from a collection of old Welsh songs, in a room which was none the worse for a portrait of Miss Maud Millett, 'The Soldier's Farewell', and the presence of a fierce-thoughted, mild-eyed young minister, who was the most majestic man I have seen since I first saw the shop-walkers at Maple's—the kind of man whom one supposes that the animals observe, and so learn to temper their contempt for us. This man had the strange whim to call the devil a gentleman, a poor distinction which I could not understand until he showed me a passage, that should be highly interesting to gentlemen and the residue of mankind, in one of the Iolo MSS. Beginning at the beginning, the MS declares that Adam's eldest son was ungenteel, 'a low vassal'; but Seth and Abel were genteel. The angels also, the tenth grade, who fell from heaven, were ungenteel, 'through pride, which is the principal characteristic of weakness'. Continuing, the writer says of Noah's sons that one was a lord, the second a gentleman, the third a servile clown. Either the usual order of the sons is changed, or Ham was held to be a gentleman because from him was descended Nimrod, and all destroyers are gentlemen. If this be true, then Japheth was a 'servile clown'—in spite of the fact that he was 'the first who made a targe with a lake in it, to signify that he and his brothers possessed the whole world', inventing heraldry—merely in order that ungentility might have a common fount. And thus we see that descent is efficacious to all except descendants of Japheth (or Ham), and that therefore the genealogies are waste paper, and a popular pursuit which has hitherto been regarded as harmless is proved to be also fraudulent. . . . Then he went back to his books, which he allowed me to see. They were pretty, uncut editions of the profane classics; theology, Welsh history, and *Grimm's Fairy Tales*—all thumbed and pencilled. Frowning above was a photograph of Spurgeon, and a picture of Whitman from a chance number of an English weekly.

When I left on the next morning early, the farmer was threshing with an oaken flail in his barn; but he stepped out to tell me what he knew of the way through the bogs and over the hills—for there was no road or path—and to beg me not to go, and to ask me to pay what I had paid at my former inn, for my lodging.

The next twenty miles were the simplest and most pleasant in the world. For nearly the whole way there was a farm in every two miles. I had to call at each to ask my way. At one, the farmer asked me in and sat me by his peat fire to get dry, and gave me good milk and butter and bread, and a sack for my shoulders, and a sense of perfect peace which was only disturbed when he found that I could not help him in the verses he was writing for a coming wedding. At another, the farmer wrote out a full list of the farms and landmarks on my way, lest I should forget, and gave me bread and butter and milk. At another, I had but to sit and get dry and watch an immeasurably ancient, still, and stately woman, her face bound with black silk which came under her chin like a stock, and moving only to give a smile of welcome and goodwill. At another, they added cheese to the usual meal, and made the peat one golden cone upon the hearth, and brewed a pale drink which is called tea. Sometimes the shrill-voiced women, with no English, their hair flying in the wind, came out and shrieked and waved directions. In one of the houses I was privileged to go from the kitchen, with its dresser and innumerable jugs and four tea-services, to the drawing-room. It was a change that is probably more emphasized in Wales than elsewhere, since the kitchens are pleasanter, the drawing-rooms more mysterious, than in England, I think. The room was cold, setting aside the temperature, and in spite of crimson in the upholstery and cowslip yellow in the wall-paper and dreary green on the floor. There was a stuffed heron; a large pathetic photograph of man and wife; framed verses; some antimacassars, and some Bibles. . . . The room was dedicated to the unknown God. The farmer did not understand it; he admired it completely, and with awe, reverencing it as a priest his god, knowing that it never did him any good, and yet not knowing what evil might come if he were without it.

Wales

St. Martin's Summer

In November I returned for a day to a lonely cottage which I had known in the summer, and all its poppies were gone. Here and there, in the garden, could be found a violet, a primrose, a wood sorrel, flowering; the forget-me-nots and columbines had multiplied and their leaves were dense in the borders; the broad row of cabbages gleamed blue in a brief angry light after rain; the black-currant leaves were of pure, translucent amber at the ends of the branches. In the little copses the oaks made golden islands in the lakes of leafless ash, and the world was very little in a lasting mist.

Yet it was not impossible to reach greedily ahead to spring, and I was doing so, in spite of the incredibly early fall of night amid the whirling and crying of lapwings, when, suddenly, a dead elm tree spoke of the summer that was past. Dead, it had been worn by the summer landscape as a memorial, as a 'reminiscential amulet'. It alone was now still the same, and strangely it spoke of the summer which it had not shared; and I recalled swiftly a night and daybreak of July.

All night we had sat silent with our books. There was no other company within a mile save that of the tall clock, with a face like a harvest moon, which did not tick, but stood silent with hands together pointing at twelve o'clock, seeming to rest, and to be content with resting, at the tranquil and many-thoughted midnight which it had so often celebrated alone until we came. But we were glad of the clock. It allowed us to measure the rich summer night only by the changing enchantments of Burton's and Cervantes' and Hudson's page, and by the increasing depth of the silence which the owl and restless lapwing broke no more than one red ship breaks the purple of a wide sea. It is a commonplace that each one of us is alone, that every piece of ground where a man stands is a desert island with footprints of unknown creatures all round its shore. Once or twice in a life we cry out that we know the footprints; we even see the boats of the strangers putting out from the shore; we detect a neighbouring island through the haze, and creatures of like bearing to ourselves moving there. On that night a high tide had washed every footprint away, and we were satisfied, raising not a languid telescope to the horizon, nor even studying the sands at our feet.

Not less strangely or sweetly than it creeps in among dreams, came in the whisper of the first swallows of the dawn among our books; and Cleopatra, the cat, slipped out through the window and left me.

But it happened that I rose and drew a curtain aside to see whether she went to the woods or to the barn. The night was over. The pool at the bottom of the garden was glazed and dim and slightly crumpled, like the eye of a dead bird; and all its willows were grim.

In the garden there was a bee. A little wind broke up the poppies petal by petal, so that they vanished like fair children in the midst of their perfections—cut off, and marked in the memory chiefly by the blank they leave, and not by an abundance such as older people entail upon us to mimic life. Hardly had I ceased to watch them than it was day. The cattle in a distant meadow stood still at the edge of their own shadows as if at the edges of pools. The dead elm tree seemed but a skull-capped, foolish jester who set a sharper edge upon our appetite for summer and the sun. The corn, the woods, rejoiced. The green woodpecker laughed and shone in his flight, which undulated as if he had been crossing invisible hedges. A south-west wind arose and rain fell softly, yet not so soothingly but that an odd thought thrust itself into my mind.

I thought of how Cervantes was not enjoying it, and in a moment I saw him and Burton and Wordsworth and Charles Lamb close by, crouching and grey, as if they had been buried alive, under knotted cables of oak root, deep under the earth which was then bearing carnation and wild rose. The wind found out the dead elm tree and took counsel in its branches and moaned, although the broad light now reigned steadfastly over leagues of shining fields.

The Heart of England

December
ﾉ❦ﾉ

Snow lightly around, yet I see spring signs: delicate new sprouts of many herbs—ground-ivy, goose-grass, nettle, wild parsnip—all pale with youth; sticky young shoots about the flaky yew-bole.

Dec. 7 1895

Cold fog and frost: the numbed, frightened birds will not leave the trees, but chirrup feebly through the curtain to one another.

Barred, sober-hued November moths cling to the oak palings, where they overlap.

Low young beeches keep their leaves whilst the tall exposed trees have been stripped.

Twin buds of woodbine opening out. Skin of the stout woodbine-stems, that cling about the oaks like rigging, is always frayed and hanging.
Dec. 11

Larks and sparrows unite their flocks.

Thrushes sing short broken melodies.

Bullfinches and wrens singly in the frost.

Fresh fronds of yarrow rising.

Loud shuffling of the blackbirds in the undergrowth.

Hazel-catkins reddening with a faint flush, like fat short caterpillars, in bunches of two, three, four, or five.

Pheasants roosting at night, very conspicuous on the bare boughs; sleep heavily and do not readily quit their perches.
Dec. 21

Wheatears linger singly in the gorse.

Wretched squatter's dwelling in the midst of a bare joyless common —rude plank shed, patched with sacks, and hedged by a mound of sods with thorns at top, and birches sheltering the cote of the pigeons, who mingle with ducks and curs within the enclosure.
Dec. 28

The Woodland Life

The Grave of Winter

When I awoke at six the light was good, but it was the light of rain.
One thrush alone was singing, a few starlings whistled. And the rain
lasted until half-past eight. Then the sunlight enshrined itself in the
room, the red road glistened, a Lombardy poplar at Kilve Court
waved against a white sky only a little blemished by gray, and I
started again westward. The black stain of yesterday's fire on the hill
was very black, the new privet leaves very green, and the stitchwort
very white in the arches of the drenched grass. The end of the rain, as I
hoped, was sung away by missel-thrushes in the roadside oaks, by a
chain of larks' songs which must have reached all over England.

I had some thoughts of branching off on one of the green lanes to the
left, that would have led me past a thatched cottage or two up to the
ridge of the Quantocks, to Stowborrow Hill, Beacon Hill, Thorn-
combe Hill, Great Hill, Will's Neck, Lydeard Hill, Cothelstone Hill,
and down to Taunton; but I kept to my road of last night as far as
West Quantoxhead. There, beyond the fountain, I entered the road
between ranks of lime trees towards Stogumber. Before I had gone a
mile the rain returned, and made the roads so bad that I had to take to
the highway from Williton to Taunton, and so saw no more of Bick-
noller than its brown tower. But I had hopes of the weather, and the
rain did no harm to the flowers of periwinkle and laurustinus in the
hedges I was passing, and only added a sort of mystery of inaccessibleness
to the west wall of the Quantocks, with which I was now going parallel. It was a wall coloured in the main by ruddy dead bracken and dark
gorse, but patched sometimes with cultivated strips and squares of
green, and trenched by deep coombs of oak, and by the shallow, winding channels of streams—streams not of water but of the most emerald
grass. Seagulls mingled with the rooks in the nearer fields. The only
people on the road were road-menders working with a steam-roller;
the corduroys of one were stained so thoroughly by the red mud of the
Quantocks, and shaped so excellently by wear to his tall, spare figure,
that they seemed to be one with the man. It reminded me of 'Lee Boo',

and how the Pelew Islanders doubted whether the clothes and bodies of the white men did not 'form one substance', and when one took off his hat they were struck with astonishment, 'as if they thought it had formed part of his head'.

By the time I reached Crowcombe, the sun was bright. This village, standing at the entrance to a great cloudy coomb of oaks and pine trees, is a thatched street containing the 'Carew Arms', a long, white inn having a small porch, and over it a signboard bearing a coat of arms and the words '*J'espere bien*'. The street ends in a cross, a tall, slender, tapering cross of stone, iron-brown and silver-spotted. Here also sang a chiffchaff, like a clock rapidly ticking. The church is a little beyond, near the rookery of Crowcombe Court. Its red tower on the verge of the high roadside bank is set at the north-west corner in such a way—perhaps it is not quite at right angles—that I looked again and again up to it, as at a man in a million.

After passing Flaxpool, a tiny cluster of dwellings and ricks, with a rough, rising orchard, then a new-made road with a new signpost to Bridgwater, and then a thatched white inn called the 'Stag's Head', I turned off for West Bagborough, setting my face toward the wooded flank of Bagborough Hill. Bagborough Church and Bagborough House stand at the edge of the wood. The village houses either touch the edge of the road, or, where it is very steep, lie back behind walls which were hanging their white and purple clouds of alyssum and aubretia down to the wayside water. Rain threatened again, and I went into the inn to eat and see what would happen. Two old men sat in the small settle at the fireside talking of the cold weather, for so they deemed it. Bent, grinning, old men they were, using rustic, deliberate, grave speech, as they drank their beer and ate a few fancy biscuits. One of them was so old that never in his life had he done a stroke of gardening on a Good Friday; he knew a woman that did so once when he was a lad, and she perished shortly after in great pain. His own wife, even now, was on her death-bed; she had eaten nothing for weeks, and was bad-tempered, though still sensible. But when the rain at last struck the window like a swarm of bees, and the wind drove the smoke out into the room, the old man was glad to be where he was, not out of doors or up in the death room. His talk was mostly of the weather, and his beans, and his peas, which he was so pleased with that he was going to send over half a pint of them to the other old man. The biscuits they

were eating set him thinking of better biscuits. For example, now, a
certain kind made formerly at Watchet was very good. But the best of
all were Half Moon biscuits. They had a few caraways in them, which
they did not fear, because, old as they were, they were not likely to
have leisure for appendicitis. Half a one in your cup of tea in the morning would *plim out* and fill the cup. They told me the street, the side of
the street, the shop, its neighbours on either side, in Taunton, where I
might hope to buy Half Moon biscuits even in the twentieth century.
The whitening sky and the drops making the window pane dazzle
manifested the storm's end, and the old men thought of the stag
hounds, which were to meet that day. . . . Just above Bagborough
there, seven red stags had been seen, not so long ago.

It was hot again at last as I climbed away from the valley and its
gently sloping green and rosy squares and elmy hedges, up between
high, loose banks of elder and brier, and much tall arum, nettle, and
celandine, and one plant of honesty from the last cottage garden. High
as it was, the larch coppice on the left far up had a chiffchaff singing in
it, and honeysuckle still interwove itself in the gorse and holly of the
roadside. A parallel, deep-worn, green track mounted the hill, close on
my right, and there was a small square ruin covered with ivy above it
among pine trees. It was not the last building. A hundred feet up, in a
slight dip, I came to a farm-house, Tilbury Farm. Both sides of the
road there are lined by mossy banks and ash and beech trees, and deep
below, southward, on the right hand, I saw through the trees the gray
mass of Cothelstone Manor-house beside its lake, and twelve miles off
in the same direction the Wellington obelisk on the Black Down Hills.
A stone seat on the other side of the trees commands both the manor
house beneath and the distant obelisk. The seat is in an arched-over
recess in the thickness of a square wall of masonry, six or seven feet in
height and breadth. A coeval old hawthorn, spare and solitary, sticks
out from the base of the wall. The whole is surmounted by a classic
stone statue of an emasculated man larger than human, nude except for
some drapery falling behind, long-haired, with left arm uplifted, and
under its feet a dog; and it looks straight over at the obelisk. I do not
know if the statue and the obelisk are connected, nor, if so, whether the
statue represents the Iron Duke, his king, or a classic deity; the mutila-
tion is against the last possibility. Had the obelisk not been so plainly
opposite, I should have taken the figure for some sort of a god, the
ponderous, rustic-classic fancy of a former early nineteenth-century

owner of Cothelstone Manor. The statue and masonry, darkened and bitten by weather, in that high, remote, commanding place, has in any case long outgrown the original conception and intention, and become a classirustical, romantic what-you-please, waiting for its poet or prose poet. I should have liked very well, on such a day, in such a position, to think it a Somerset Pan or Apollo, but could not. It was mainly pathetic and partly ridiculous. In the mossy bank behind it the first woodsorrel flower drooped its white face among primroses and green moschatel knobs; they made the statue, lacking ivy and moss, seem harsh and crude. Some way farther on, where the beeches on that hand come to an end, two high stout pillars, composed of alternate larger and smaller layers of masonry, stand gateless and as purposeless as the king, duke, or god.

For a while I rested in a thatched shed at the summit, 997 feet up, where the road turns at right angles and makes use of the ridge track of the Quantocks. A roller made of a fir trunk gave me a seat, and I looked down this piece of road, which is lined by uncommonly bushy beeches, and over at Cothelstone Hill, a dome of green and ruddy grasses in the south-east, sprinkled with thorn trees and capped by the blunt tower of a beacon. The primrose roots hard by me had each sufficient flowers to make a child's handful.

Turning to the left again, when the signpost declared it seven and three-quarter miles to Bridgwater, I found myself on a glorious sunlit road without hedge, bank, or fence on either side, proceeding through fern, gorse, and ash trees scattered over mossy slopes. Down the slopes I looked across the flat valley to the Mendips and Brent Knoll, and to the Steep and Flat Holms, resting like clouds on a pale, cloudy sea; what is more, through a low-arched rainbow I saw the blueness of the hills of South Wales. The sun had both dried the turf and warmed it. The million gorse petals seemed to be flames sown by the sun. By the side of the road were the first bluebells and cowslips. They were not growing there, but some child had gathered them below at Stowey or Durleigh, and then, getting tired of them, had dropped them. They were beginning to wilt, but they lay upon the grave of Winter. I was quite sure of that. Winter may rise up through mould alive with violets and primroses and daffodils, but when cowslips and bluebells have grown over his grave he cannot rise again: he is dead and rotten, and from his ashes the blossoms are springing. Therefore, I was very glad to see them. Even to have seen them on a railway station seat in the rain, brought from far off on an Easter Monday, would have been something; here, in the sun, they were as if they had been fragments fallen out of that rainbow over against Wales. I had found Winter's grave; I had found Spring, and I was confident that I could ride home again and find Spring all along the road. Perhaps I should hear the cuckoo by the time I was again at the Avon, and see cowslips tall on ditchsides and short on chalk slopes, bluebells in all hazel copses, orchises everywhere in the lengthening grass, and flowers of rosemary and crown-imperial in cottage gardens, and in the streets of London cowslips, bluebells, and the unflower-like yellow-green spurge. . . . Thus I leapt over April and into May, as I sat in the sun on the north side of Cothelstone Hill on that 28th day of March, the last day of my journey westward to find the Spring.

In Pursuit of Spring

Bibliography

BOOKS BY EDWARD THOMAS

1897   *The Woodland Life* (William Blackwood and Sons, London)

1902   *Horae Solitariae* (Duckworth, London)

1903   *Oxford* (A. & C. Black, London)

1904   *Rose Acre Papers* (S. C. Brown Langham, London)

1905   *Beautiful Wales* (A. & C. Black, London)

1906   *The Heart of England* (J. M. Dent, London)

1909   *Richard Jefferies* (Hutchinson, London)

1909   *The South Country* (J. M. Dent, London)

1910   *Rest and Unrest* (Duckworth, London)

1910   *Rose Acre Papers:* including Essays from *Horae Solitariae* (Duckworth, London)

1910   *Feminine Influence on the Poets* (Martin Secker, London)

1910   *Windsor Castle* (Blackie and Son, London)

1911   *The Isle of Wight* (Blackie and Son, London)

1911   *Light and Twilight* (Duckworth, London)

1911   *Maurice Maeterlinck* (Methuen, London)

1911   *Celtic Stories* (The Clarendon Press, Oxford)

1911   *The Tenth Muse* (Martin Secker, London)

1912   *Algernon Charles Swinburne* (Martin Secker, London)

1912   *George Borrow* (Chapman & Hall, London)

1912   *Lafcadio Hearn* (Constable, London)

1912   *Norse Tales* (The Clarendon Press, Oxford)

1913   *The Icknield Way* (Constable, London)

1913   *The Country* (B. T. Batsford, London)

1913   *The Happy-Go-Lucky Morgans* (Duckworth, London)

1913   *Walter Pater* (Martin Secker, London)

1914   *In Pursuit of Spring* (Thomas Nelson and Sons, London)

1915   *Four-and-Twenty Blackbirds* (Duckworth, London)

1915   *The Life of the Duke of Marlborough* (Chapman & Hall, London)

1916   *Keats* (T. C. & E. C. Jack, London)

1916 *Six Poems* (The Pear Tree Press, Flansham, Sussex)

1917 *A Literary Pilgrim in England* (Methuen, London)

1917 *Poems* (Selwyn & Blount, London

1918 *Last Poems* (Selwyn & Blount, London)

1920 *Collected Poems* (Selwyn & Blount, London)

1922 *Cloud Castle* (Duckworth, London)

1926 *Essays of To-day and Yesterday* (George G. Harrap, London)

1926 *Chosen Essays* (The Gregynog Press, Newtown, Montgomery-shire)

1926 *Edward Thomas*, The Augustan Books of Poetry (Ernest Benn, London)

1927 *Selected Poems*, edited by Edward Garnett (The Gregynog Press, Newtown, Montgomeryshire)

1927 *Two Poems* (Ingpen & Grant, London)

1928 *The Last Sheaf* (Jonathan Cape, London)

1928 *Collected Poems* (Ingpen & Grant, London)

1936 *Collected Poems* (Faber and Faber, London)

1938 *The Childhood of Edward Thomas* (Faber and Faber, London)

1938 *The Friend of the Blackbird* (The Pear Tree Press, Flansham, Sussex)

1940 *The Trumpet and Other Poems* (Faber and Faber, London)

1948 *The Prose of Edward Thomas*, selected by Roland Gant. With an Introduction by Helen Thomas (The Falcon Press, London)

1949 *Collected Poems* [fifth impression] (Faber and Faber, London)

1962 *Selected Poems*, edited by Robin Skelton (Hutchinson, London)

1965 *Selected Poems*, edited by R. S. Thomas (Faber and Faber, London)

1965 *The Green Roads*, edited by Eleanor Farjeon (The Bodley Head, London)

1965 *Four-and-Twenty Blackbirds*, with illustrations by Margery Gill and a Foreword by Helen Thomas (The Bodley Head, London)

1974 *Collected Poems* [eleventh impression] (Faber and Faber, London)

1977 *Diary of Edward Thomas 1 January–8 April 1917*, with Introduction by Roland Gant, Foreword by Myfanwy Thomas, Woodcuts by Hellmuth Weissenborn (The Whittington Press, Andoversford, Gloucestershire)

1977 *Edward Thomas: Complete Poems*, edited, with Introduction and Note, by R. George Thomas (Oxford University Press, London)

A SELECTED BIBLIOGRAPHY OF BIOGRAPHICAL AND CRITICAL WORKS

1935   Thomas, Helen. *As It Was . . . World Without End* (Heinemann,
        London)
1937   Guthrie, James. *To the Memory of Edward Thomas* (The Pear
        Tree Press, Flansham, Sussex)
1937   Eckert, R. P. *Edward Thomas: a Biography and a Bibliography*
        (Dent, London)
1939   Moore, John. *The Life and Letters of Edward Thomas* (Heinemann,
        London)
1956   Thomas, Helen. *As it Was and World Without End* (Faber and
        Faber, London)
1956   Coombes, H. *Edward Thomas* (Chatto & Windus, London)
1958   Farjeon, Eleanor. *Edward Thomas: The Last Four Years* (Oxford
        University Press, London)
1962   Scannell, Vernon. *Edward Thomas* [Writers and their Work]
        (British Council/National Book League/ Longmans)
1968   Thomas, R. George (ed.) *Letters from Edward Thomas to Gordon
        Bottomley* (Oxford University Press, London)
1970   Cooke, William. *Edward Thomas: a Critical Biography* (Faber and
        Faber, London)